Outdoor Education

for

American Youth

PREPARED BY AAHPER COMMITTEE

UNDER CHAIRMANSHIP OF

JULIAN W. SMITH

Associate Professor, Outdoor Education
Michigan State University,
and Director, AAHPER Outdoor Education Project

AMERICAN ASSOCIATION FOR HEALTH
PHYSICAL EDUCATION, AND RECREATION
Washington, D. C.
1957

Price: $2.50

Preface

J UST ten years have elapsed since the publishing of the May 1947 issue of THE BULLETIN OF THE NATIONAL ASSOCIATION OF SECONDARY-SCHOOL PRINCIPALS, which was devoted to "Camping and Outdoor Education." During this ten-year period, outdoor education has assumed an ever increasing importance until today it stands as one of the most significant developments in education.

There are many reasons why progressive school administrators are devoting increasing attention to outdoor education. In this age of expanding leisure, millions of people are seeking the out-of-doors. Unfortunately, thousands of them will be denied the full measure of enjoyment of outdoor experiences because of the lack of basic attitudes, knowledges, skills, and appreciations. Most of these basic requisites for enjoyment of the out-of-doors can be learned and developed through a sound school program of outdoor education. Thus the school has a vital responsibility for equipping every boy and girl with these attitudes, knowledges, skills, and appreciations which are so essential for lifelong enjoyment of the out-of-doors.

Because of their deep concern for the role which secondary schools should play in the development of outdoor education programs, the National Association of Secondary-School Principals and the American Association for Health, Physical Education, and Recreation, both departments of the National Education Association, have cooperated in preparing this publication. An attempt has been made to incorporate the best thinking of outdoor education leaders and school administrators who have been responsible for developing successful programs in various parts of the country. At the same time, an attempt has been made to cite as examples only those programs which might conceivably be duplicated by other school systems desiring to use these examples as patterns for the development of their own programs. Thus we feel this material will be especially helpful to school administrators, boards of education, and other professional and lay leaders sincerely interested in the development of outdoor education.

PAUL E. ELICKER
Executive Secretary, NASSP

CARL A. TROESTER, JR.
Executive Secretary, AAHPER

Acknowledgments

THE material included herein represents the cooperative efforts and contributions of a number of people. Special acknowledgment is made, however, to the following members of the Planning and Editorial Committees who served as coordinators for specific chapters:

JULIAN W. SMITH, Director, AAHPER Outdoor Education Project, College of Education, Michigan State University, East Lansing, Michigan (*Chairman,* Planning and Editorial Committees, and *Coordinator* for Chapters 3 and 5); JACKSON M. ANDERSON, Assistant Executive Secretary and Consultant in Recreation and Outdoor Education, AAHPER, Washington, D. C. (*Coordinator* for Chapter 4); REYNOLD E. CARLSON, Professor of Recreation, Indiana University, Bloomington, Indiana, and HARLAN G. METCALF, Director of Recreation Education, State Teachers College, Cortland, New York (*Coordinators* for Chapter 2); JOHN DODGE, Conservation Educator, New Hampshire Fish and Game Department, Concord, New Hampshire (*Coordinator* for Chapter 1); and L. B. SHARP, Executive Director, Outdoor Education Association, Inc., New York, New York (*Introduction*). Written material for the various chapters was contributed by the following:

Chapter I. *The Setting and Need for Outdoor Education*

1. "The Shape of Things To Come" by JOHN E. DODGE
2. "Outdoor Education and the Curriculum" by EARL C. KELLEY, Professor of Secondary Education, Wayne University, Detroit, Michigan
3. "The Community School Theory and Its Implications" by G. ROBERT KOOPMAN, Associate Superintendent, Department of Public Instruction, Lansing, Michigan

Chapter II. *Outdoor Education in the High School Program*

1. "The Secondary School Subjects" by GEORGE W. DONALDSON, Director, Camp Tyler, Tyler, Texas; and MILTON J. GOLD, Associate Professor of Education, Hunter College, New York City
2. "Settings for Outdoor Education" by LESLIE S. CLARK, Director, Sargent Camps (Boston University), Peterborough, New Hampshire; JULIAN W. SMITH; REYNOLD E. CARLSON; FRANK WALTER, Director of Outdoor Education, Roslyn Public Schools, Roslyn, New York; WALLACE HAWKINS, Head, Agriculture Department, Tyler High School, Tyler, Texas; and GEORGE W. MARTIN, Registrar and Director of the Evening School, Olympic College, Bremerton, Washington
3. "Enriched Living Through Outdoor Experiences" by GUNNAR PETERSON, George Williams College, Chicago, Illinois; PAUL M. KOTILA, Principal, Graveraet High School, Marquette, Michigan; JACK F. GEORGE, Director of Health, Physical Education, and Recreation, Roslyn Public Schools, Roslyn, New York; CLIFFORD L. NETHERTON, First Vice-President,

Table of Contents

CHAPTER I

THE SETTING AND NEED FOR OUTDOOR EDUCATION

CHAPTER II

OUTDOOR EDUCATION IN THE HIGH SCHOOL PROGRAM

CHAPTER III

FACILITIES AND RESOURCES FOR OUTDOOR EDUCATION

CHAPTER IV

TEACHER PREPARATION

CHAPTER V

A LOOK INTO THE FUTURE

* * * * *

Introduction

OUTDOOR Education is a common sense method of learning. It is natural; it is plain, direct and simple. The principal thesis which underlies the implications of outdoor education for all subject matter, in all areas of study, and at all levels is:

> *That which can best be learned inside the classroom should be learned there.*
>
> *That which can best be learned in the out-of-doors through direct experience, dealing with native materials and life situations, should there be learned.*

This realistic approach to education rests squarely upon the well-established and irrefutable principle of *"learning by doing."*

Scientific research and psychological testing have been going on for many years to determine how learning actually takes place. Not only was the Dewey theory of "learning by doing" established as sound; it was also proved that through direct experience, the learning process is faster, what is learned is retained longer, and there is greater appreciation and understanding for those things that are learned at firsthand.

Thus it becomes crystal clear that much of what is called for in the standard curricula of the public schools can most effectively be learned in the out-of-doors. Moreover, learning in the open is a mutual process. In the classroom, subjects tend to become artificially separated from one another, as do pupils from teachers. Regaining touch with the real world leads to their becoming reunited. People and things are seen in their true relationships; facts and ideas that are most important emerge in perspective.

While school camping is not synonymous by definition with outdoor education, it rests on the same premises and is recognized as one of the forerunners in its development. It furnished the laboratory in which testing could be done, processes refined, leadership identified. Experiments were conducted which related camp learnings to the progress of the camper in school. Results were conclusive—and amazing.

More than a decade ago we conducted further experiments to see whether some learnings could be achieved more quickly and effectively in a favorable school camp environment than in the classroom. Scientific testing used in these experiments did prove that the camp setting was more effective for certain learnings. The outcome of these significant findings and the pilot programs which followed went far to establish the validity of outdoor education.

Today, outdoor education, including school camping, is accepted as an integral part of the total school program. Few administrators doubt its vital role in the curricula of their schools. It is generally accepted that every school youth should have, as a regular part of his school experience, opportunity to adventure and explore—thus solving for himself some of the questions posed by life outdoors.

Educators believe it is good for our boys and girls to experience at firsthand something so direct, so plain and simple and natural. Perhaps that is why as you turn the pages that follow, you will find them documenting more than half a hundred plans by which American schools are now seeking to fit outdoor education into their existing patterns. They are committed to a principle and to a way of life.

L. B. SHARP

CHAPTER I

The Setting and Need for Outdoor Education

1. THE SHAPE OF THINGS TO COME

HARASSED administrators are conditioned to resist the advances of myriad special interest groups that clamor for the inclusion of new programs in their already bursting curricula. Rightly, they demand to know "why?" even before challenging "How can we do it?" Recreation skills—angling and casting, firearms training, camping, small craft and water safety, skiing, mountaineering—the list seems to grow longer every year. Where are they to draw the line?

Nowadays, educators readily concede that boys and girls who are to become constructive citizens must learn to use resources wisely. There must be problem solving in the real world of their own community with which these youngsters are most familiar. They must taste success which comes with achievements valid by adult standards. If these experiences are to be other than vicarious, they must use the actual terrain where the problems exist as their laboratory.

But what of these other activities that seem at first glance unrelated to the recognized workload of the public schools?

Not until we are prepared to accept the term *Outdoor Education* strictly at face value does their true place in the pattern of total education emerge. This is not another discipline with prescribed objectives like mathematics or science; it is simply a learning climate which offers special opportunities for direct laboratory experiences in identifying and resolving real-life problems, for acquiring new skills with which to enjoy a lifetime of creative recreation, for attaining attitudes and insights about working with other people and getting us back in touch with those aspects of living where our roots were once firmly established.

The Changing Scene in American Life

Last year, more than thirty million Americans bought licenses to hunt and fish.

In 1955 over ninety million persons visited our national parks and forests.

In 1956 more than twenty-five million licenses to operate small craft were sold in this country.

Figures like these document one illuminating fact. *Today, more of our nation's citizens seek recreation in outdoor environments than through*

1

any other single channel that allows them full and active participation. As individuals they run the entire gamut of ages from eight to eighty. Neither sex predominates.

The astute school man will not let himself be sidetracked into sterile debate as to whether recreation is a legitimate concern of education. He knows full well that it is his job to turn out boys and girls equipped both as individuals and as members of a social group to adjust and contribute to the complex society in which they will find themselves launched. Most areas of education serve to enrich the recreational life of the individual, while sound recreation involves activities that further the development of the whole person and are thus an integral part of his education. Moreover, education of this sort is something that will tend to persist and grow after he leaves school for the rest of his natural life.

Rather the educator will turn perceptive eyes upon the *quality* and *environment* of recreational opportunities to which his charges are being introduced and for which they will be equipped. If he sees them stimulated to seek and enjoy emotional outlets in which they can take an active, even a creative part, then these will be judged of the highest order. In evaluating these outlets, he will give due weight to the job setting in which today's youth is destined to find itself, for the significance of recreation is not merely to satisfy a need for play nor to provide a pleasant excuse for doing nothing. Ideally, it will include all-absorbing activities *that contrast sharply with the surroundings of one's working life,* so that he will be drawn out of himself to emerge later refreshed and regenerated. Thus environment is an all-important factor in identifying what are worth-while recreational experiences for each of us.

The Shift to the City

This trend to give first priority to recreation in outdoor areas may then be attributed to healthy intuition on the part of the American public; for figures from the Bureau of the Census indicate that by 1950 almost sixty-four per cent of our people were living in urban situations, while it has been said that today seventy-five per cent of our youngsters go to school in the city.

Before he thought, the principal of a large urban high school might say: "Well, there's one thing I certainly don't have to worry about. Camping and outdoor living are nothing my students need learn!" How long can America's educators afford to remain in an ivory tower?

If these boys and girls in the big city schools are to emerge as well-integrated people and take the new era in stride, they must be prepared. Granting the wealth of opportunities their curriculum now offers, they still face the nation's toughest problems of mental health and adjustment for they are caught up in the very vortex of emotional strains and pressures and unrelenting pace of modern living. They lack the natural checks and balances and reference points which are the birthright of the country dweller.

As they go on in life, does their principal anticipate that *all* the bonanza of new-found leisure time to which our age has fallen heir will be constructively taken up in the music and art and civic pursuits for which he has so richly equipped them? Are they to be content with watching television or other spectator sports, or should they be trained to participate? Does he know of any team sport which will serve them all their lives? Realistically, won't they head out of town in ever-increasing thousands for more and more weekends and vacations that demand the skills of outdoor living and recreation—just as their parents are now doing?

New Ways Not To Grow Old

Projecting these implications for a lifetime of healthy living, there is another phenomenon of the current era that we cannot neglect—increased longevity. Back in 1900 the average man used to die at forty-six years of age and the average woman at forty-eight. In 1954, they lived to be respectively sixty-seven and seventy-three. Even this increase in average life span by more than twenty years does not make the point so dramatically as conservative insurance company tables, which give a person who has reached the age of fifty a life expectancy of 21.37 more years to spend on this earth!

This miracle of medical science, accomplished chiefly during the past two decades as infant mortality and epidemics came under control, is no more breathtaking than medicine's new approach to keeping active those who have reached the older age brackets. Just as they now discharge surgery cases from the hospital in days when it used to take weeks, any doctor will tell you that he regards it as sound therapy to keep his older patients in better health for a longer time for them to engage in absorbing activities, even though this may necessitate his administering drugs to overcome specific disabilities. So closely is the health of their bodies linked to their mental and emotional tone that these will actually remain in better physical condition through purposeful use than through disuse.

Remember that this is existing practice for men of science whose ethical code commits them to keep human bodies functioning despite almost any social sacrifice. It places a high premium indeed upon education which will equip each youngster with skills and attitudes and understandings that open avenues of creative recreation suitable for his declining years. For these things are not learned by most of us after we once become adult, and it is the rare and lucky individual who still finds himself in the autumn time of his living fully occupied with job or career. Yet within the next decade or two, new trends will impinge upon our society that are destined to increase many fold these years of leisure for the average American.

Social Outcomes of the Push-Button Revolution

Labor unions and industry have furnished the facts, but they alone appear to be duly concerned. It may conservatively be stated that within the next ten years, millions of hours of additional leisure time will be the inevitable by-product of the push-button revolution we call *automation*. By 1965, a work week that *lasts only four days* will be a reality for a large segment of our people.

While it is clearly not a function of this report to explore *all* the educational implications of automation, two questions raised by the C.I.O. are directly pertinent:

"Will the nation's educational, cultural, and recreational facilities be capable of meeting the challenge of increased leisure made possible by automation—longer vacations, reduced work weeks, two and a half or three day weekends?"

"Will power and natural resources be sufficient to meet the potential increased output made possible by automation?"

Thus, from another angle we see brought into sharp focus the twin areas of concern for education which demand access to outdoor laboratories—recreation and conservation. In order to grasp clearly what is implied, it may be pertinent to re-identify three types of technological development that actually serve to define automation, since loose talk and misinterpretation have beclouded its meaning:

1. *Integration*—the linking of conventionally separate manufacturing operations into lines of continuous production through which the product moves "untouched by human hands."

2. *Feedback*—the use of control devices or servo-mechanisms that allow individual operations to be performed without necessity for human control.

3. *Computing Machines* (like Univac) —capable of recording and storing information, and of performing both simple and complex mathematical operations on such information.

It is evident that these three concepts reduced to practical application imply revolutionary changes in personnel requirements, both for industry and for business giants, such as the telephone companies with their dial systems, utilities, banking, insurance, and a host of others. Not only will they mean that fewer man hours accomplish more production, but they will also vastly alter the working life and emotional needs of the individual. Old incentives will become meaningless and new ones will take their place. At a premium will be the alert, technically trained "service" man, concerned with watching dials and correcting mechanical failures, rather than operating machines himself. He will be carrying immense responsibilities and using his brains all the time. His productive working life will presumably be shorter, as well as his work week. Yet his pay checks and benefits will place him in a strategic position to provide himself and his family with transportation and recreation on a scale hitherto undreamed of.

For the men and women of this new "working class" in America, the enjoyment of outdoor areas for weekend recreation, vacations, and retirement will become a primary and meaningful incentive, even more so than is now the case for our professional groups.

People Plus More People Build Cities

As we have already noted, Americans are fast becoming a race of city dwellers, but there is another relentless trend in our society which of itself literally *makes* cities. To grasp its import, we have only to look at the new housing developments around almost any urban center.

Bureau of the Census experts predict that by 1975, our present population of 167 millions will have risen to at least 221 millions—an increase of over 7,000 more people living in this country each day!

Up to this point we have been discussing social implications for workers who make up the base of our economic pyramid—in big business, industry, the floating populations that move from factory to factory, the supporting occupations of cool miners, railroad men, and the like. But it is inevitable that workers in the various service trades who supply their needs and are dependent upon their payrolls will soon be drawn into the same urban vortex of living conditions. Even our farmers become relatively fewer each year as their individual production is increased through scientific practices and applications of automation. Marginal producers are forced out and must seek jobs in the city.

If we look squarely into those seven thousand new faces a day, we can discern among them the many who live to an older age, the voting majority who have never made firsthand acquaintance with the land and resources upon which their very existence depends, the floating populations of people who lack real roots anywhere, the universal and imperative need for constructive use of leisure time to rebalance perspective.

It is small wonder that return to the outdoors is now taking on the dimensions of a great national movement.

Implications for Conservation and Education

Thus it becomes apparent that all the trends we have discussed serve merely as preamble to resolving the sort of social problems which conservationists and educators must face together—for they are paramount to the welfare of our free society. Unless democracy through this sort of teamwork can find effective means for coping with them, America faces attrition of her resources, both human and natural, which can lead only to tighter Federal controls or to fundamental national weakness.

The impact of this ever-growing flood of recreation-bent city dwellers upon our remaining outdoor areas becomes the direct concern of the conservationist, for he is committed to promote the *wise* use of natural resources by people. What if new millions descend like Attila's horde of old, untrained but armed to the teeth with every type of equipment and gadget that a modern sporting goods store can furnish? What will they do to our national heritage of forests and lakes and rivers, our fishing and hunting, our peaceful countryside—even though they come to play! What will they do to each other—morally and physically? Anyone who has watched a gang of youngsters play in a deserted building will know the answers!

This in itself is one of the critical problems with which conservation education must deal, and one which to date has been least widely recognized as such. But there are others implicit in the situation; pyramiding populations plus increased ability to pay are destined to make stupendous demands upon our hard-pressed natural resources. Of these, admittedly wildlife is recreational in character, but soils, water, forests, minerals, and the remainder of the animal kingdom are of primary utilitarian significance. Government estimates indicate that by 1965 our national income will be fifty-two per cent higher than it it today. More people spending more money mean very simply that we must have more intelligent use of our resources if these are to stand the strain.

Now that most of our citizens have become divorced from firsthand experience in managing these resources, yet are still instrumental in sucking them dry, how can we expect to insure their conservation through democratic process? There seems to be no adequate answer except to reacquaint people, and particularly our youngsters, with the issues at stake. While much good background can be developed in the classroom, it appears to be the consensus of informed opinion that, to result in desirable behavior changes, this must be fortified with direct experience in the field.

High-school boys and girls, impressionable, altruistic, and believing as they do that black is black and white is white—with no room for a gray zone of alibis or excuses, feel that their schools owe them this opportunity for significant community and national service.

Our Coefficient of Failure

In contrast with seven and one half million boys and girls now enrolled in our nation's high schools, more than one million have dropped out.

Breaking down these drop-outs by age classes, it proves that about one half of the sixteen to seventeen year old group are without jobs, guidance, supervision, or direction, while in the fourteen to fifteen year old group that ratio rises to over two thirds! It is small wonder that delinquency runs about ten times as high among the drop-outs as among those boys and girls who stay in high school.

Now these one million lost youngsters are not merely a problem in themselves. They are the symptom of a greater problem. They point up with inexorable clarity the inadequacy of traditional high-school offerings to meet the needs and challenge the abilities of that docile herd of captives which remains within the school's walls, presumably through inertia or following the urge to conform.

No one in his senses will advocate outdoor education as a panacea for curing all these ills, but it is one of the most logical and promising tools modern educators are learning to use as part of the process. It can make a significant contribution to meeting the needs of millions of boys and girls our high schools are now losing—in whole or in part.

Pioneers, Oh Pioneers

Lincoln Steffens once pointed out with rare perception the superior status achieved by his *"Boy on Horseback"*—how self-assurance and security were the product of rediscovering this primitive proof of command over environment that lifted one mentally as well as physically above his fellow man.

This is but a symbol of one sort of experience needed to round out the modern person. For most of us who have lived to become mature adults, our quota consists in a mosaic of minor incidents spread out over time and space, *but each one did something to make us whole.*

*　　*　　*　　*　　*

I remember a storm-tossed night alone on a mountain lake, so black and rain drenched that no beam of light could pierce the murk. My small boat pitched and wallowed down each trough to be eased back up the next crest lest it swamp completely. A seeking wind gusted from the northeast to drive spray and rain needle-like into my left cheek. And therein lay the secret: keep the wind in that quarter for a constant bearing to reach camp and security. At seventeen I knew no apprehension, only exultant confidence in a strong arm and expert boat handling to bring me in—as in due course they did.

*　　*　　*　　*　　*

Three youngsters crouched around the site of last night's camp fire. A foot of rotten snow still lay in the woods, and it had been raining for twelve hours. Their sodden bedrolls had been partially protected by canvas, but everything else in this country of northern softwoods was drenched through and through.

Abruptly, one of the boys rose and trudged off silently through the slush till he reached the trunk of an ancient Canadian birch, long since dead. Moments later a tiny flame from his lighter flickered against the heavy flakes of bark, died, flickered again and began to mount as the oil ignited. He dared not breathe while part of his soul climbed with that tenuous flame to support it in its supreme effort. When it stabilized and he fed it faggots with tender care, his two companions leaned closer until they were knit as one with him in the warmth of the growing fire.

*　　*　　*　　*　　*

At 4:30 the sun rose over Idaho. It touched Baker and the other volcanic peaks with that lambent shade of rose the Spaniards named Sangre de Christo. *Below us lay a cloud bank a couple of thousand feet thick that cut us off from earth as completely as if we were on another planet. A hundred feet above, dormant fires that smolder in the bosom of Ranier sent wisps of smoke curling gently upward through the eternal snows that blanket her summit.*

During the night we'd climbed from Camp Muir upward through Godiva Gulch, clinging with our crimpons to the steep ice walls, listening for the dread trickle of rock that warns of avalanches which hurtle down that worn gulley with scarcely time for you to jump.

Now we stood alone on the glacier that shrouds one of the world's great peaks. There were a crevasse or two still to be negotiated, but all real danger lay behind and below. We belonged to a special fraternity.

*   *   *   *   *

Each of us can perhaps look back and cite a variety of occasions on which he was privileged to joust with primitive forces and to win his spurs, but what of today's adolescents to whom society may unwittingly deny this fundamental human right? Are we so certain that those we now stigmatize as delinquents were not simply victims of a misdirected urge for adventure and self-establishment far better met by making available such opportunities? Might not many of our "docile sheep" who drift along into drab anonymity suddenly come to life as effective citizens when they had thus rubbed horns with reality in the raw?

50 Million Private Car Owners Can't Be Wrong

In this age of air travel it is commonplace to observe that our world has shrunk, but less frequently recognized is the fact that communities have extended their bounds to a like degree. For a community's limits must be identified by the area required to service the living needs of its people, both physical and emotional.

Out of the very core of our push-button urban society rises a phenomenon of central significance—the family automobile. Americans now own more than 50 million private cars. This is no mere evidence of individual opulence nor of business necessity; it is a symbol of new-found freedom of soul for city dwellers. Over ever-increasing networks of super highways, these millions of motor cars are putting on mileage to create a new concept of community geography.

As you ride through the night past unending rows of suburban homes that surround some strange city, think twice before you rank their occupants as helpless captives of their environment. Behind many a lighted window lies a stack of road maps and atlases ready at hand.

This is the stuff that dreams are made on. For one, there is the vision of that incredible silver torrent plunging down from the sky named Yosemite; for another, the herds of elk and mule deer, the moose and grizzlies and lesser citizens that room at large in Yellowstone. It may be ancient cave dwelling which have hung in the canyons and draws of Mesa Verde since the days of Columbus, or a canoe questing down some foam-flecked river among spruce forests of the Adirondacks or Quentico-Superior. Perhaps it is just the nostalgic smell of a bow bed or the hiss of skiis over packed powder snow on a high trail—the loveliness of the Smokies in rhododendron time, or a herd of antelope skittering across the plains while a fresh wind blows clouds off the Bighorns.

These things are as much American as baseball or baked beans or television. When the average citizen can reach out for them by piling his wife and his kids and his cat in the car and taking off half-way across the country, there is nothing unrealistic about thinking of your community as stretching out a couple of hundred miles and perhaps across state lines. In fact, that may be where you will find yourself standing, dwarfed by the generators of some huge power dam which spans your own river and brings lights to the very city in which you live, when you trace these back to their source. Up there at head waters lie the beginnings of your community milk shed and the farms that bring you food, as well as the flood control structures and sustained yield forests which safeguard your economy.

Two Different Worlds?

It would be manifest nonsense to set a double standard that recognized one set of meanings and experiences as the measure of our adult community, and another for its community school. Clearly, this poses problems for which public education as we know it today must find answers. It is demonstrable, however, that their resolution, rather than necessitating the addition of still more courses to an already over-crowded curriculum—just patching up the plumbing as it were—will exercise a unifying influence in the continuing process of curriculum revision to meet the accepted imperative needs of high-school youth in our free society.

Teamwork from the national right down to the local community level is providing invaluable support for the schoolman from both groups and individuals. Outdoor education can supply him with a climate of learning in which vital experiences touch off chain reactions that lend new meanings and motivations to the entire program which his high school offers its youngsters. So, when the wheel has turned full circle, these boys and girls will find every hour of their waking lives all year round caught up in a series of adventures that make sense because each is targeted toward completeness of growing up under adequate guidance and direction. It is they who will be the pioneers of tomorrow's America.

2. Outdoor Education and the Curriculum

THE central institution for the development of our youth is the school. This is the one place where we all pool our resources so that the young may be helped to grow into adequate human beings. The older notion—that the function of the school was merely to impart knowledge—will no longer suffice. It will not suffice because the conditions under which our young are forced to grow up have changed. Our society is so compact and complex that unless the school sees itself as the youth agency in our society, the simplest needs of our young will not be met.

If the school sees itself as society's central agency for youth, this will be a change in role from that of merely imparting knowledge. This change, I believe, will be in the direction of meeting new conditions that already have taken place in society. If the schools do not become the agency for youth, then it seems certain that a competing agency will be set up. Never again will this nation allow its youth to deteriorate as in the early part of the last depression, when we had hundreds of thousands of boy and girl tramps on the highways of our country. When this condition arose during the early thirties, two Federal youth agencies were formed to meet the problem. Most of us remember the C. C. C. and the N. Y. A. We did not get rid of these agencies until the advent of World War II; and it is my opinion that if we had not become involved in war, we would still have them, and they would be doing most of the youth work today.

I do not mean to criticize these agencies as they functioned. Something had to be done for our youth who had no place in school or at work. The school found its resources curtailed, and in some respects became a less effective instrument than it had been before. The N. Y. A. gave our youth something constructive to do and a little money they could call their own. The C. C. C. was a gigantic outdoor education enterprise.

I do not believe, however, that a Federal agency is the proper place for these services. We worry about Federal control of education if a few dollars are appropriated by Congress for school buildings, while we run the risk of again turning over a large part of our job to the Federal government by default. In May 1950, just before the Korean war broke out, a bill was introduced in Congress to reactivate the C. C. C.; and so it will be again at the first slackening of employment and prosperity, unless the school sees itself as the proper agency for furnishing these services.

The need for a change in the role of the school from that of imparter of knowledge to that of the broader youth agency has been caused by three major changes in our society. They are (1) *urbanization,* (2) *mass education,* and (3) *new research in the nature of learning.*

The Shadow of the City

It is well known that in the last fifty years we have ceased to be primarily a rural people and have become mainly city dwellers. A large city is not a good place in which to raise children. We will not all move back to the farm on this account, and so we have to do what we can to make the urban setting more tolerable for our young.

By living in cities, we have deprived our children of room to grow up. It takes a certain amount of room for children and youth to have the things to do that bring about growth. This lack of room is a limiting factor even in our best city homes. It is particularly critical in some of our low-income homes.

We have deprived our youth of the land and of the development that comes from living intimately with the earth from which we spring. We have deprived them of the opportunity to assume real responsibility. Learning to be responsible was automatic in the rural situation because it was apparent to all that if everyone did not work, there would not be enough to eat. It is not possible on a 40 foot lot to find enough real tasks for three or four children to learn responsibility.

Once a wealthy man who lived on an estate sought to furnish responsibility to his son by buying a cow for the son to care for—clean the barn, feed and milk the cow, and sell the milk. This the boy did for a while, although he knew that his father could buy a whole herd of cows and hire a man for each cow if he wanted to. The boy knew that the whole thing was phony. He was saved from open rebellion by the intervention of the health department which stopped him from selling the milk.

Some people are inclined to blame parents because our youth do not seem to be as responsible as they were when good people like you and I were young. They even say that parents do not love their children as they formerly did. There is no evidence that human nature has changed, or that parents no longer love their children. We might ask ourselves how we would teach responsibility if there were five of us living in one room with an alley for a playground. Parents have not changed, but the conditions under which they have to rear children have changed.

Youth is entitled to an opportunity to learn to be responsible. This can happen when he has a task that is real, that needs to be done, and that is worth doing. Since this cannot be supplied in sufficient quantity in the urban home, the problem must be met in the school. This fact has many implications for the curriculum.

A New Role for the School

The fact that mass education, where nearly everyone, rather than a selected few, comes to school, demands a new role for the school. I believe education for all is the noblest experiment! Never in the history of mankind has so large a nation offered so much education to so many. It is our country's attempt to make all citizens—even the least of us—literate, informed, and equipped with skills enough to participate in our democracy and to help make it work. It is our recognition of the fact that a democracy cannot survive with an ignorant electorate.

When everybody came to school, however, many problems were created. We had a well-established curriculum which had developed when the secondary school was intended for the few who wanted to enter one of the professions or who had at least shown an aptitude for book learning. The classical curriculum, made up of "solids," was not just well entrenched; it had in many cases become sacred. With some people, any attack upon, or even concern about, this curriculum was sacrilege. It was as though the "solids" were not man-made, but had been handed down from on High.

When all American youth came to school, there were many who not only did not want this curriculum, but were also not able to understand a word of it. These were good American citizens, but different. Since we could not change our student body, it seemed that we would have to change the curriculum.

This we have done in part and regretfully. We have resorted to patch work; we devised many courses that are not "solid," but which serve as good places to stand some youth while the real education went on for the others in the regular courses. We could not dispose of all our new people in this way, so we watered our subject matter down, thinned it out. In some places we tried a new approach for the learners, whereby we attempted to fit the school activities to the needs, interest, and abilities of the individual child. This effort, though it seems sensible, has been small in comparison to the whole. For the most part, the original curriculum, in form, if not entirely in substance, has withstood the onslaughts of the multitude. It has proved itself to be one of the most static features of our culture during the time when the rest of the world has changed so much that it is scarcely recognizable.

I believe that adopting education for all has had more impact on the schools than any philosophy or any of the perennial arguments about what the schools should be doing. Teachers and administrators have tried their best, in most cases, to hold the academic line in the face of an onslaught. They are subject to criticism, not because they have not tried heroically to hold the line, but because they have not changed their basic position in a changing culture.

What We Now Know About the Learning Process

In addition to being beset by urbanization and mass education, researchers have been probing into the nature of learning and how it takes place. Many of the new findings, arrived at by scientific method, tend to show that even when we had the small school with the selected student body, our teaching methods were not in keeping with the best ways of learning.

We know now that one learns in the light of his own experience, and that he cannot learn without experience. We used to think the learner was simply perverse if he did not learn what we thought he should.

The individual learns best when he is involved in what is to be learned —when he has been consulted and has at least given consent to the enterprise. This involvement needs to be in the thing itself, not for some outside reason, such as a grade or graduation.

This means that the student learns best when he is ready to learn—not necessarily when the class comes to the chapter in the book. Being ready simply means what has been said above. He gets ready by gaining the experience needed to have something to hitch onto, and by becoming involved. Readiness does not mean willingness. He may be ever so willing, but he cannot learn without adequate previous experience and maturity.

The student learns best when his total organism is involved—when he has an opportunity to do more than look at a book and engage in purely mental activities. Not that he cannot learn anything from a book, but the amount of learning and retention is limited if there is no further involvement.

It is easy to see how these new findings in the nature of the learning process play havoc with the materials and methods of the old school. It is very difficult to teach the far-away, the obscure, the abstract to most young people. None of the old methods, where knowledge is set out to be learned, conforms to what research tells us about learning.

A Real-Life Climate for Learning

Many problems have beset secondary education. A changed role, vast numbers, students unsuited to the offerings, lack of facilities, need for changed methods—these will doubtless make the teachers welcome the advent of outdoor education and school camping. Outdoor education is not now a large part of any school program, but it is already established in a good many places. It has proved its worth. Enough records have been kept so that a respectable account of what has happened is available.

Let us consider some of the values of outdoor education through school camping, which seem to be one of the most effective means, although many of the values are present in other outdoor settings. A class or group of children go to a campsite where they live together, eat together, sleep in cabins, and explore the outdoors together. They are accompanied by their teacher who becomes a part of the life thus lived. So far, this plan for outdoor education, like many of the other good things of life, has been, to a great extent, part of the elementary, rather than the secondary, program. The high schools have had some experience with it, and it is hoped that they will have more.

There is great value in the subject matter learned in the camping situation. It is good for city youth not only to be told how to plant a tree, conduct a fish survey, or build a bird refuge, but also actually to do these things. *It is the involvement of the total organism,* so valuable for learning at its best. To contrive such a learning situation in the classroom is difficult.

Implication for Citizenship

There are other learnings, however, which I believe far exceed in value the mere learning about the outdoors, important as this is. Here youth has an opportunity to *learn cooperation in an entirely new dimension.* This is an important lesson for urban youth, who live in a society so close-knit that it is the most cooperative in the history of mankind. The closer people live together, the more important it is that they learn to cooperate. In the camping situation, the need to take one's fellows into account is so obvious that we do not need to preach about it. The dormitory, the kitchen, the dining room, the recreation—all require the cooperation of everyone. This is not abstract; it is not idealogical; it is simply there. A situation exists; it is not invented. Cooperation has a survival basis in the camp which is more difficult to accomplish in the classroom. Learning how to relate one's self with others is probably the most important learning one can have for our modern culture. One scarcely can do anything these days without the involvement of other people.

With cooperation comes *responsibility*. Again this is automatic—makes sense—in the camping situation. Problems and tasks do not have to be invented—no cows have to be bought—to make the tasks real. If the members fail to carry out their responsibilities, the group simply does not eat, sleep, or play. This is the way responsibility was taught before we became urban. If it appears that youth is not as responsible as in the days of yore, it is due to the fact that they have not had the same opportunity to learn responsibility.

Usually a group establishes a form of self-government which not only highlights the lessons in responsibility, but also gives *experience in democratic control.* Through this device, youth, themselves, establish the rules under which they will operate. Having established the rules themselves, they are not inclined to break them. In camp, I have seen young people deciding what rules to follow with regard to smoking, dining-room etiquette, at what time lights should be out at night, and many other items. I have also seen boys who were considered to be delinquents in the city become cooperative and even assume constructive leadership roles in an outdoor environment.

If there are those who think that youth, given an opportunity, will not construct a good society, we have ample evidence that this is not so. We have seen proof, again and again, that youth desires a good society as much as adults. If they err, it is on the side of being too strict with themselves. When youth break rules, it is the other person's rules that are broken, not those which they had a hand in making. In this, youth are very much like adults. We, too, have a tendency to disregard rules made by someone else and in which we have no part.

Youth, in camp, get a *new concept of freedom,* where freedom within the social situation is achieved. Youth do not want to do "just as they please." This is a low-level freedom, which they see will not work when other people are involved. If they wanted this low-level freedom, they would not make rules of conduct. The camping situation gives them a natural opportunity to learn that freedom in the form of license to do "as they please" is limiting in its nature. They learn that, by giving up freedom to do "just as they please," they achieve freedom on a higher, more effective level.

Roots of Our Culture

A great and rather undefinable value in outdoor education is that the city youth gets an opportunity *to relate to the earth and sky.* City youth seldom see anything that is not man-made. Sidewalks, curbs, streets, buildings are all in straight lines, but nature never uses a straight line. Even the parks are laid out and planted according to man's notion of what nature might devise. Research does not reveal what it is that causes man's spirit to expand when he comes in contact with the earth from which he sprang. No one who has ever seen a sunset or felt the warm earth of spring under his feet can deny that something enhancing to human development exists here. This is doubtless the reason the deer hunter, the trout fisherman, or the bird shooter gets a wild look in his eye at certain times of the year and hies himself to the woods. He does this at enormous cost to himself in money and discomfort.[1] He eats food he would not touch at home, sleeps under conditions he would ordinarily consider torture. It is not for meat that he does this, although he may stoutly deny this statement. "Progress" has long since settled this matter for all of us. Modern man can get better meat, and more of it for the money within a few blocks of his home. It is rather the call to nature and to the earth that spurs him on. And he is glad—counts it worthwhile —even though he brings home no game and is pained in body and in purse. He has satisfied a yearning beyond pain.

So it is with the city youth. We have observed personality changes for the better when city youth encounter and commune with the earth. There is no substitute for this in the city situation. Many thousands of our city youth never get the opportunity to know what communing with nature means. Sometimes research may be able to tell us more about what happens when one gets an opportunity to relate himself to his earth, but that changes do occur seems indisputable.

Outdoor education in a camp setting need not be as expensive as it appears at first glance. Many school plants are now being built. Part of the plant could be at a nearby place where woods and water are available. We have to begin to think of the school as serving the needs of youth before we can see a different school plant. With planning, both in building and in curriculum, the program could be devised so that the campsite is an integral part of the school system. The outdoor program, then, would be carried on with the camp operating as just another part of the school plant.

I see outdoor education as significant because it is a part of the curriculum. It takes place on school time. It provides opportunity for returning something to children that has been taken away by urbanization. It is in keeping with modern research on the nature of the human organism and of learning. It gives some opportunity for city children to see the earth, to live cooperatively and democratically, and to learn to assume responsibility. It even provides an opportunity to live creatively for a time. And I believe that creative living is the best way to learn how to be a part of a changing world.

---

[1] For a really adequate statement on what our sportsmen will endure, see "Back to the Bush," a chapter of *Literary Lapses* by Stephen Leacock.

This school, adjacent to a park area, provides excellent opportunities for outdoor eductaion.

3. The Community School Theory and Its Implications

Modern Education Has Stressed Formalism

THE idea of "school" is irrevocably linked in the modern mind with "formal education" rather than with "complete education" or with "human growth and development" or with "better community living" or with "community development." The very list of alternative connotations is shocking. Laymen and professionals alike normatively respond to "school" in much the same way. Even the present-day products of our best schools of education are usually prepared only to administer a school of formal education. Their virginal ignorance of any other concept of school or school program is a logical result of their upbringing.

Formal education, as it is known in the modern world, is a post-renaissance concept based on a modern philosophy. From the time of the emergence of Western Europe from the Dark Ages, western man has been concerned primarily with becoming universally literate. The representatives of the universal western church under the Papacy and, later, the reformers following Luther and Melancthon have brought western civilization to a high level of literacy. The written word, whether it appears in the Holy Book, the novel, or the science textbook, is no longer the possession of privileged classes such as the clergy, the educators, the writers, and the rulers.

This emphasis on literacy and formalism has left its mark. The completeness that characterizes most systems of tribal education has been lost. Formalism has been over-emphasized. Even people interested in education in the out-of-doors often feel that they must formalize their procedures unduly. A field trip or a camping experience is a complementary (not a supplementary) experience to the experiences that a given pupil has in the classroom. It is merely an expression of completeness in education.

Formal Education Tends Toward a Narrow Concept of "School"

Adapt or perish! This principle of adaptation is half understood by both peasant and savant. But it is not always applied. This decade is witnessing the passing of a generation of rural fathers and mothers who have parented urban children. Like the mother hen who sets a clutch of duck eggs, these parents don't know what to do about the offspring. Boy Scouts, Cub Scouts, Bluebirds, and Little Leaguers are the results. The school is as much at a loss for a line of action as are the human parent and the mother hen.

Adaptation in the anthropological sense may seem to be an academic issue—but it is hardly that today. Kaleidoscopic social and technical changes indicate that a race for survival is on. Survival of the citizen and of the United States of America is discussed in every newspaper in this country every day. Survival kits are essential equipment for the housewife as well as for the soldier. There is even erroneous talk of "survival education"—another abusive cliche.

The Community School Theory Met a Philosophic Need

No people ever entered an emergency more unprepared than were Americans in 1930. Both individuals and institutions were caught unawares. The school as an institution was unprepared. True, it had broadened its curriculum in the ten preceding years, but it was not community oriented nor was it oriented to change. Out of the emergency came a new and useful adaptation of educational theory. It was seen that education should be oriented to the realia and conditions of a community. Here was a concept having to do with the *purposes, administration, and services* of a school big enough to meet the need. This concept gave and is still giving life and broad purpose to the modern American school system. The community school theory represents a major philosophic advance for modern education the world over.

Specifically, this broad cultural concept of "school" makes way for a complete education for each individual rather than a narrow, partial, mechanistic education such as is represented by a narrow interpretation of formal education or an equally narrow interpretation of vocational education represented by the apprentice education given to the educationally under-privileged today.

Those interested in the "extended classroom"—a good community school term—should rejoice over the recent development. The community school creates the climate and the opportunity for education out-of-doors or for anything else that is good and wholesome in education.

The Community School Operation Is Based
on Physical Resources, People, and Skills

A community is based in one sense or another on land, water, and other physical resources. It also has a technical system based on knowledges, skills, and tools. The individual, young or old, is concerned with learning to operate the technical system and to live with it in all of its implications. In one sense, people are in themselves the chief resources of a community—hence the importance of growth and development.

Community School Administration
Is Cooperative Administration

The typical community has a multiplicity of agencies. These agencies have many resources and programs. The school as a major agency is in a key position because its chief business is learning—and it is learning that begets community development. Gradually—and, indeed, rather rapidly in recent years—the need for cooperative planning and coordinated operation has been recognized. Lewis R. Barrett has pioneered in community planning and coordination as is indicated by a number of his survey results. The American Academy of Social and Political Science[2] has produced a scholarly analysis of the problem. A multi-disciplinary group has helped produce a guide.[3] *The School Executive* has produced an ex-

---

[2] The American Academy of Political and Social Science. *The Annals—The Public School and Other Community Services.* Volume 302, November 1955. Philadelphia 4: The American Academy of Political and Social Science, 3937 Chestnut Street.

[3] Koopman, G. Robert. *My Town.* East Lansing, Michigan: G. Robert Koopman, 625 Butterfield Drive. March 1956.

cellent model.[4] Multi- disciplinary groups of scholars are increasing. Examples of partial coordination abound in American communities. The essential principles of cooperation have been clearly recognized. Those interested in fields such as education out-of-doors should feel free to move forward on the wheels of cooperative planning.

The Community Curriculum Is Based on
Adequate Categories of Opportunity

The concepts of *the community curriculum* and the corresponding *categories of opportunity* are essential to a cooperative community program. The former may be defined as *"the community curriculum or the sum total of all of the planned and contrived learning experiences of the community, of the impact of all of the natural and man-made resources of the community, of all of the supervised education, recreation, and group work in the community.* It refers to all of the creative learning experiences of the people of a community. It is a community curriculum in the sense that it grows out of the needs, interests, resources, and conditions of the community. It is a curriculum, thus it is *planned* within minimal limits. It is planned and thus it requires a marshalling of resources and facilities, each one in relation to the other."[5]

The categories of opportunity are broad and range from:

"1. The opportunity to participate in a broad, thorough, systematic, and continuing education program"

to

"9. The opportunity, for growing boys and girls particularly, to be associated together in a life in the outdoors and learn the skills associated with this type of living, and learn of the habits and beauties of nature through contact with them and with the aid of organization and leadership peculiarly fitted to this purpose."

Program Planning Is the Crux of the Process

Creative program planning is essential to any activity. Such planning should involve all of the agencies involved on a friendly, helpful basis. Such planning is difficult to achieve, but in its absence the competitive, wasteful process of programming is bound to develop. Such programming results in the waste of the community dollar and the deprivation of the most needy individuals. Every community survey uncovers much such waste and deprivation.

Extending the classroom into the out-of-doors demands the use of many resource people and many physical facilities. It seems axiomatic that such programs should be based on cooperative planning.

Cooperative planning cannot proceed without data about need. Such data should in this instance be arrived at by the cooperative action of many agencies. They should be pooled in the process of creative program planning. The data should range from needs of children of all ages to the needs of families and organized groups. Too often community programs in the camping and similar fields are based on the "baby sitting" philos-

---

[4] Random Falls.
[5] Koopman, G. Robert. *op. cit.*

ophy. The vitality and interest being shown by young families indicate the need for programs which will help them to participate with their children in outdoor activities. Such programs should be carried on by adult education centers and recreation staffs and will mean a whole new area of development in many communities. In others, such as Flint, the models for such programs already exist.

Cooperative Planning, Construction, and
Use of Physical Facilities Are Essential

As programs and facilities have proliferated, donors, taxpayers, and members of control boards have become more cognizant of the need for cooperative planning and action. Planning commissions, conservation departments, schools, cities, and voluntary agencies have recognized that, in forward planning, communities can no longer afford anything but full use of physical facilities. Park schools are already a reality. Millions of acres of public lands and parks have been made available to community agencies. While it is still desirable for some agencies such as schools, churches, foundations, and youth agencies to own properties of their own, the vast burden of programs is being thrown more and more on *commonly used public facilities*. It is high time that the community dollar be protected from waste in the form of private preserves and darkened school facilities.

Again the only process to be called upon is the cooperative community committee supported with enough resources to secure research data and professional consultation service. In fact, every community should have a long-range committee in this area to assist local authorities and planning commissions and to promote coordination. To date, the engineer and the architect have been forced to build facilities largely from their own ideas due to the failure of program people to do adequate functional planning.

Programming and Staffing Is a Cooperative Process

Programming should be done in terms of the individual child or adult to be served. This principle is demonstrated beautifully in the Random Falls idea, a reprint of an article that appeared in *The School Executive* (March 1956). In actual programming there are two grand phases or processes; namely, (a) making the program plan for a community and (b) the continuous adjustment of the program to the individuals and aggregates of individuals involved. Here it is seen again that coordination is the heart of the process. Community experiments in which staffs from various agencies have provided day-to-day and week-to-week coordination have been very revealing and encouraging. The laboriousness of this process often keeps people from it, but such coordination still must be recognized at the test of any good community program. The problems of initiative, of hegemony, of dominance, and of paucity of staff are real problems and each must be dealt with firmly. In the last analysis these problems will diminish in proportion to the growth of a philosophy and practice of cooperation.

The Basic Staff Should Be Provided by Public Agencies

The problem of provision of a basic staff is fundamental. Again, as in the case of physical facilities, the trend is toward having public agencies with access to the equalizing tax dollar provide the basic or nuclear staff. No rigid scheme will work since the individual agency such as a Boy Scout organization has a unique function to perform. Churches make a unique contribution to human growth, development, and stature. However, many of the means for carrying out responsibilities can best be provided by specialists or by teams of staff members. For example, it seems obvious that a YMCA camping activity would involve many staff people including volunteer parents, group work internees, the sanitarian from the public health agency, the representatives of the park department, the community school specialist in physical education and recreation, and, of course, staff from the sponsoring agencies. The same principle could apply to either field trips or church picnics.

Public Participation Provides a New
Basis for Relationships and Programming

The so-called problem of public or community relations practically cares for itself under the community school theory. Interpreting, selling, and propagandizing are largely replaced by participation. A group of parents that participates in an evening volley-ball class for several years is almost certain to insist that plant and facilities be included in a new secondary-school building. The additional cost will be provided. Ends and means become closely associated in democratic living.

As in the case of community relations, the cooperative community program can be lifted from an entertainment level where evaluative data consist of the number of persons attending ball games to the creative level. Once inducted into the process, almost any citizen will thrill to the opportunity to build a new world for the adults and children of tomorrow. Children and teachers who have built a bridge over a stream in a school forest will not be the same thereafter either in their interests or their relationships. Teenagers who have explored James Bay in a canoe are more apt to become interested in geo-physical research than to become comic book readers and shuffleboard players.

As has been previously indicated, a co-planned community program of learning will deal with all ages. The school and other youth-serving agencies will, through planning, come to recognize the needs of other groups. Families will be stimulated to do a better job of education for their constituent members. No cooperative community will ever need a congressional committee in Washington to urge it to build a program for its potential delinquents. No properly organized community will fail to see the needs of the aged and aging. The ghastly tragedy of the passive pensioners awaiting the grave should be a challenge to everyone to build programs of education and recreation for people of all ages.

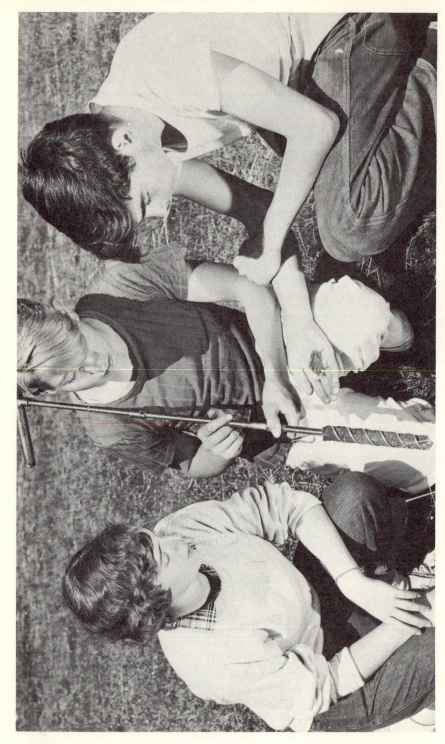

Eight inches of the most precious substance in America—topsoil.

CHAPTER II

Outdoor Education in the High School Program

1. RELATING OUTDOOR EDUCATION TO HIGH SCHOOL SUBJECTS

WITH certain notable exceptions, the adoption of the methods and materials of outdoor education has moved slowly in the secondary schools. Doubtless the very enormity of the administrative problems of time and space accounts for a large measure of this reluctance. However, American schools, at all levels, have taken justifiable pride in their ability to make the necessary administrative adjustments when they are convinced of the need for newer methods or materials. Witness the time and place modifications made necessary by such courses as distributive education, driver training, and vocational shop. Or, note the temporary schedule changes and travel arrangements made to facilitate the playing of a game of football, basketball, or baseball.

American secondary schools have adequately demonstrated their ability to live with—and profit by—a flexible schedule. They have likewise shown that they can move teacher and pupils to the point at which the desired experience can be had. It may well be said, then, that administrative problems constitute a challenge, or even a quite difficult obstacle, but not a valid excuse for failure to provide secondary-school students with the vivid learning experiences which await them outside the classroom.

If secondary-school teachers, supervisors, and principals *want* to do the job, it can be done. Possibly the fact that so few of them do want these rich experiences for their pupils traces directly back to their own lack of understanding of the richness of the outdoor environment. Teachers who have not, as high-school or college students, experienced the thrill of direct experience learning in the outdoors need help in pin-pointing the relationship of the outdoors to their own teaching areas.

No brief document such as this can hope to explore all of the possible relationship between secondary-school subjects and the outdoors. Only some of the more obvious ones are cited herein. Creative school people will discover many, many more.

Conservation and Outdoor Education

Some people like to say that conservation is the "subject matter" of extended outdoor experiences. Participation in a democratic community, the *living* experiences of students working, studying, and playing together

—these are *method*. Conservation provides something worth while, necessary, and challenging for students to work on and study about. Conservation determines the nature of the recreation which will be available in leisure hours for future years.

What are some of the criteria for viable outdoor education experiences for secondary-school youth?

1. They must provide genuine *learning* opportunities.
2. They must capture the youth's imagination as being worth while.
3. They should provide for growth of the concept of social service—of a contribution freely made for the betterment of the community.
4. They should require constructive work on the part of the student to develop the concept of social service, to provide some work experience, most of all to secure—through personal involvement and contribution—a sense of commitment to the conservation of our natural heritage.
5. They should be real, not simulated, experiences.
6. They should be well-rounded, not reflecting premature specialization.

Academic and Laboratory Goals

What are the goals of such experiences? A comprehensive, detailed view of the natural resources picture? No, but a general understanding of man's dependence upon well-managed, interrelated natural resources. A sharp distinction has to be made between academic study experiences that can develop informational objectives economically and efficiently, and first-hand laboratory experiences in which the main goal is to develop a technique in approaching resource problems, an attitude, a sense of commitment.

The two methods bolster each other. It is a mistake to use one process where the other would be more effective. The student may study types of conifers in a classroom, using printed materials, projected images, samples, and other devices—and develop a meaningful store of information in this way. But the sense of commitment to conservation is established not in this manner, but in the morning or afternoon in which Johnny or Betty and their classmates reseed a hillside which for some reason is not reseeding naturally. Firsthand experiences in the "forest primeval" are necessary to get the feeling of Longfellow's phrase.

Does this mean that attitude-building is the only contribution that the outdoor laboratory makes to conservation education? The answer lies, of course, in the nature of the program to which the outdoor learning situation is contributing.

Objectives Adapted to Goals

The needs of some classes will be general. The social studies teacher will perhaps be more interested in attitudes and understanding—in the sense of well-being that springs from wise use, of desolation from poor use; in the understanding of cooperative efforts among the resource-users, private organizations, state, and Federal agencies; in the necessity for societies to insure the preservation of their resources. The language arts teacher is interested in natural resources as a source of inspiration, as background and stimulation for reading, as material both for reports and for creative writing. Music and art find similar uses.

In some fields teachers will have objectives that are more specific in nature—that are more directly informational. The science teacher is interested in values derived from firsthand impressions of flora and fauna—in tree identification and growth cycles, in the interrelationship of resources, in environments that are conducive to plant growth and animal survival, in developing a background of reality against which he may later project detail and understanding through vicarious sources. The agriculture teacher wants his class to see how a field is laid out to make the best use of contours. He wants them to note the effects of a grassed waterway. He wants to show the effects of overgrazing, of the use of cover crops, of good drainage systems. The forestry teacher wants his class to have experience in cruising, in planning a sale, in planting, thinning, or pruning. The conservation or general science teacher wants to show the effects of block and selective cutting of timber on wildlife and the planning in a watershed for interrelated resources.

The nature of the need determines the type of experience to be provided. The more general the purpose, the more valuable the extended experience. Where attitudes and understandings are paramount, the need for exposure is greatest. The boy or girl with no direct immediate concern needs time to "browse" in the outdoors, to have guidance in studying the rocks and rills, woods, and templed hills in person. The camp-type experience makes this unhurried, extended exposure possible. Being able to *do* something about it and working to improve the resources give the added meaning, the significance and purposefulness which the secondary-school student requires.

Science

Biology teachers have probably used the outdoors more, and more systematically, than any other teachers. Unfortunately, only a small percentage of this group realize its value.

It is axiomatic in the world of living things that plants and animals are part and parcel of the environment in which they live. Biological facts and principles are poorly understood, if at all, when living things are viewed out of their environmental context. The frog in formaldehyde that so many students have studied is quite unlike the frog on the banks of the creek. The pickled frog has structure but no function; he has no need for food, or protection, or propagation. And these very aspects of his life are what make him a frog. A sound and true understanding of frogs cannot result from such isolated study. How much better it would be to combine the traditional textbook and laboratory work with enough field work to assure an understanding of the frog "in context"!

Environmental studies do not constitute the sole justification for outdoor experiences in biology. Collection trips are another rewarding use of the outdoors. Organized and supervised collection trips can result in much finer things than a mounted collection. Too often, students making individual, unsupervised collections have contributed materially to the destruction of the very things they should be learning to understand, admire, and conserve.

Biology field work to observe seasonal changes also offers rich possibilities. The enormous amount of biology subject matter relating to the field of resource use need only be mentioned here because it is amply documented in the references that follow (see chapter V).

Chemistry teachers might well use field trip techniques in the outdoors when dealing with such problems as chemical elements in soils, community sanitation, and domestic water supply. Teachers of secondary-school physics have frequently used the outdoors, especially when the area of light is related to astronomy and telescope construction. In school camps, many of the basic tools and processes of woods work are among the most simple illustrations of the laws of physics. For example, the use of a cant hook or peavey to roll logs is a clear cut and meaningful illustration of the lever principle.

In the field of vocational agriculture, teachers have rather consistently employed the outdoors as instructional material. Whether in "projects" on the students' own farms or, as is increasingly true, on farms owned and operated by the school, students actually do farm work, planning, and bookkeeping on school time in the outdoors.

School farms and school forests are dealt with more elaborately in another section of this document. Suffice it to state here that school-owned farms and forests serve a three-fold purpose as related to the high-school curriculum: (1) demonstration of good farm practices in the over-all farm program, (2) laboratory observations of specific farming procedures, and (3) actual participation of the students in farm work.

Social Science

Alert social science teachers have long used the methods of outdoor education. Trips to a ghost town or an abandoned farm can give high-school students of history or modern problems a keen insight into the changing patterns of America's development. An hour or two spent at an excavation site can demonstrate more clearly than thousands of words the slow, tedious methods by which much of history is literally dug out.

A bus trip through a farm area can illustrate the problems faced by American farmers. The sight of eroded fields and muddy streams can point up the social importance of one of America's great problems—wise use of our natural resources.

Secondary schools that have access to a camp are fortunate. In camp, the social science teacher can actually build the kind of social environment about which he is teaching. Students can plan and "live" a pioneer day or can, in the day-to-day scheme of camp living, practice pure democracy, representative democracy, or—to illustrate its disadvantages—possibly a period of anarchy or dictatorship.

Physical Education

The field of physical education with its allied fields of recreation and health probably has more opportunities in the outdoors than any other curriculum area. Whether its immediate objective is that of healthful exercise and fun for its present value or that of providing students with life-long recreational skills, outdoor activities provide a simple and economical answer. Here are invigorating activities in which the student can find challenge now and in which he can engage as long as he lives. Here are wholesome activities for the individual and ones in which his whole family can participate—now and in the future.

A number of secondary schools have approached outdoor education through the rather simple device of adding instruction in the skills of casting and shooting. These activities are almost ideal in that they fit neatly into existing administrative structures and are not prohibitively expensive. Simple instructional procedures in fishing and hunting enable youngsters to begin, safely and efficiently, recreational activities that are life-long in value.

The formation of Outing Clubs in junior and senior high schools appears to offer other great values. Such clubs, long a valuable addition to the college scene, have been largely ignored in the public schools. In outing clubs youngsters learn the simple skills of hiking, outdoor cookery, and general comfort and "at-homeness" in the outdoors.

Family camping, while almost totally unorganized and, by its very independent nature, a poor subject for systematic, scholarly study, appears to be the major recreational development of our age. Literally millions of Americans are flooding public camp sites every summer in quest of cheap, simple outdoor recreation. Outing clubs provide instruction in the skills so sadly lacking among too many family campers.

One of the real puzzles to an observer outside the physical education field has been the almost total lack of attention by physical educators to that one physical activity in which almost everyone engages almost every day of his life—walking. Possibly hiking clubs—or simply walking some place while in physical education classes—promise an answer. Americans, emotionally tied to automobiles as they are, don't walk enough. And they are missing one of the most relaxing and best conditioning exercises there is. It is logically the job of physical education to re-open this most simple and healthful activity of all to youth.

Language Arts

On the surface, there appears to be little or no relationship between language arts and the outdoors. A closer look, however, reveals a real and needed function of the outdoors in teaching youngsters efficient and creative use of language. Teachers of composition have long known that a pupil must have real experience, experience which has meaning to him, before he has anything to write. Even the most imaginative writer starts with something real. Directed outdoor observations, possibly in connection with other courses, can provide this needed reality. Teachers of language arts might well make use of the experiences pupils have had on, say, a biology field trip or an outing club hike to provide the subject matter for descriptive writing.

The outdoors has, since mankind first wrote words, provided much of the finest of inspirational, creative writing. The alert teacher of literature or composition shares this rare experience with his pupils. Just as the art teacher takes his pupils outdoors to get vivid, impressive firsthand experience, so will the imaginative teachers of language go outdoors with his pupils for inspiration. It's there for the asking.

Arts and Crafts

Secondary art pupils will find in the outdoors, in class-hour excursions, or on extended trips a wealth of visual impressions. The translation of these impressions into the various art forms could readily become the very center of instruction in the graphic arts.

Materials found in the outdoors—clay, grasses, interesting forms in knots or driftwood, dried flowers, or seed pods—the list is endless—can add breadth and depth to the secondary art courses, which have too often been simply offerings in drawing and painting. The discovery of beauty everywhere and the creation of beauty from even the unbeautiful might well be the objectives of taking art outdoors.

Mathematics

Geometry, that branch of mathematics which had its beginnings in an outdoor problem—re-surveying the Nile Delta after the yearly floods—probably provides the most meaningful relationship between mathematics and the outdoors. Actual use of geometric principles in surveying, measuring, and estimating can add life and reality to a sometimes dull subject. The history of mathematics is one of mankind's most thrilling achievements. By taking pupils back where the problems first existed—on the land—the creative teacher can share the heroic past with today's students. And, as a bonus, he will get meaningful insights impossible with regular textbook instruction. Geometry can become a thrilling exploit into the environment instead of dreary "learn-it-because-you'll-need-it-some day" routines.

Modern youngsters, reared away from the land, have but hazy notions of our common measures such as yard, rod, mile, or acre. These are real problems in the outdoors. The pupil learning to use map and compass deals with them in a situation charged with reality. Estimates begin to come easy when there is real need for them.

Homemaking

Homemaking cuts across a number of subject areas when it deals with the outdoors. The simple example of that great American pursuit—backyard cookery—illustrates the point. Here is cooking, clearly in the home economics area, blended with relaxing fun, just as clearly in the area of recreation. And, if the family wants to be creative about it, it can project into geography and history by experimenting with outdoor dishes of other lands and times. It can design and build its own barbecue pit or smoke oven, thus impinging upon industrial arts.

If the teacher of homemaking is interested, as certainly she should be, in providing instruction in wise and healthful family use of the outdoors, she will deal with problems of proper shoes and clothing for hikes, picnics, or family camping trips. She may even go to the next step and explore with her pupils problems of economical, well-balanced, and easily transported food. Shelter, beds, and bedding also constitute legitimate and interesting problems to be solved.

An interesting possibility in the field of homemaking is that of designing a number of outdoor "home projects" for the students. One of homemaking's major objectives is that of "fostering better family relations." What better way is there than that of helping the family to better ways of family recreation through outings, picnics, backyard cookery, or even family camping trips?

Core Curriculum

All of the above has assumed the traditional subject matter organization of the high-school curriculum. In those schools that have departed from such organization, the initiation of outdoor education should prove an easy task. The broad-area organization of subject matter that is characteristic of the core curriculum and its large time-block scheduling are both favorable to outdoor activities.

Outdoor problems seldom fall neatly into a given subject matter area. Most often they cut across two or more areas. Curriculum organization that is problem centered can deal with such multi-subject problems with a great deal more facility than can the more generally known subject-matter organization. It is probably for this reason that outdoor education and school camping have been more warmly received by core curriculum schools than by others.

Co-curricular Activities

In addition to the various curriculum areas cited above, attention should be directed to that area of secondary education that is least bound by traditions, as time and space problems, co-curricular (or extra-curricular) activities. Conceived originally as a broadening or enrichment feature of the school offering, this area lends itself most readily to the expansion and development of outdoor activities. The very fact that many co-curricular activities are scheduled outside the school buildings and after school time makes for the much wanted flexibility. A partial list of the possible organizations are: hiking club, outing club, bird watchers, outdoor chefs, astronomy club, telescope builders, and gardeners.

Outdoor education offers opportunities for a variety of co-curricular activities.

Teacher-Pupil Relationships

One of the significant benefits that comes to teachers and pupils who share in the vivid and adventurous experiences that outdoor education offers is that of a better understanding of each other. All too often, the teacher is viewed by his pupils as a bookish, sedentary person. A teacher who sees his pupils only in the classroom can just as readily conceive of them in a single-faceted manner. The many sides of personality which are almost automatically drawn out when teachers and pupils share a real experience may never be seen in the more restricted atmosphere of the classroom. Home-room teachers and guidance counselors, as well as the pupils' subject matter teachers, could benefit from such relations. This is the "bonus" factor in outdoor education for secondary-school youth.

Outdoor education in the secondary school is still largely an unexplored and uncharted area. It remains a challenge to adventurous teachers and administrators. There can be no doubt that great values are inherent in it for secondary-school youth. Neither can it be said that the job cannot be done. What else do American schools need?

2. SETTINGS FOR OUTDOOR EDUCATION

USE of the outdoors for more specific learning activities may involve either extended experiences or field trips of relatively short duration. Much depends upon the area in which the school is located and the resources that are available within easy traveling distance. Often large cities find the extended experience necessary for all such activities, since too much time is taken for transportation alone on the shorter field trip. In some cases schools maintain their own farm or forest within easy distance of the school. Sometimes part of the school site has been planned as an area for learning about natural resources. In other instances a location remote from the immediate school community has compelling values to recommend its selection. School camps have proved one of the most effective and practical means of making such outdoor learning opportunities available.

School Camping

For almost two decades camping has been or become a part of the educational system in many communities. The number of school camps is increasing steadily. Stimulated by pilot programs by Life Camps, Inc.— now the Outdoor Education Association—and by local and state experimental ventures in Michigan, New York, and Washington and aided by the W. K. Kellogg Foundation, upwards of five hundred school districts in half the states now use camps for learning experiences in the outdoors; for it has been clearly proved that certain learnings can be acquired more quickly and effectively in a favorable camping environment than in school.

A number of schools have year-round operations, while many more use camps for several weeks throughout the school year. While the greatest growth has been in the elementary schools, an increasing number of such camps are reported at the secondary level. There are now enough documented experiences of this type of outdoor education to make it relatively easy for high schools to initiate pilot programs in most sections of the country. Consultant services and materials are available from national and state professional organizations, state departments of education and conservation, universities and colleges, camping agencies, and other organizations to assist schools in school camping ventures.

As a result of much experimentation and evaluation, some principles and guides can be stated that will be helpful in setting up new school camps and in improving present practice.

1. The school camp must be a part of the total school plant. No modern school will be complete unless it owns or has use of a large tract of land for year-round outdoor education activities.

2. The camping activities must be an integral part of the total school program and operated by the superintendent and teaching staff under the auspices of the board of education.

3. Cost of operating the school camp should come from school funds the same as for any part of the school program.

4. Wherever possible the school camp should be planned to serve the community.

5. In selecting a campsite, it is important to secure a large enough tract of land to provide not only for the camping program, but also for other phases of the outdoor education program. Schools may need to purchase their own property or may make arrangements for use of county, state, or Federal land.

6. Standardization of camp structures should be avoided.

7. Individual growth and development takes place best when campers are divided into small groups of seven to ten each for participation in the many camp experiences.

8. In most parts of the country, living quarters will need to be winterized. During warm seasons and in some parts of the country, living quarters can be in canvas-roofed types of shelters, many of which can be constructed by campers and staff.

9. The school camp has a unique opportunity to bring about total educational growth of youth through small group living and through putting them into close touch with their natural surroundings.

10. The camp program should be planned by the teachers and students. It is best to use the small group process in planning and carrying out the program. This program would include arrangements for living, menu making, food marketing, cooking, sharing

of all duties and work, meeting weather conditions, maintenance of shelters, forestry, conservation, and many kinds of trips and explorations.

11. The camp program must emerge naturally out of the local school situation and must be planned and conducted so that:
    a. Every camper participates.
    b. Each camper has the opportunity to discover himself, his place in his small group, his contribution to it and to gain better understanding of how people live and share together.
    c. Its content is centered in the out of doors; it should give campers a fuller understanding of our natural resources and how to use them, and teach them to solve some of their own problems connected with man's basic needs for food, clothing, shelter, group living, and spiritual uplift.
    d. It is motivated by causing campers to do for themselves and solve their own problems; and to use nature materials effectively and according to good conservation practices.

Initiating a Program

The initiation of a school camping program is not unlike other curriculum innovations. Creation of an outdoor education committee composed of representatives of the teaching staff, students, and citizens has been found effective. Whatever study plan be envisioned, preparations should include the following:

1. Securing information concerning other outdoor education programs through publications, films, and visitations if possible.
2. Making an inventory of community resources available for leadership, materials, and facilities.
3. Studying community interests and needs to determine how school camping can make a unique contribution to the curriculum.
4. Recommending a plan of action to the school administration, beginning with a proposed pilot program.
5. Selecting one or more classrooms or activity groups for the pilot effort where there is already interest and readiness on the part of students, teachers, and parents.
6. Providing inservice training for prospective staff members through visitations and workshops held at the setting for the camp.
7. Making careful pre-camp planning with both students and parents concerned in the classroom groups involved, and making full use of available consultants.
8. Setting the stage for interpretation and evaluation of the pilot program as a basis for determining a long-range plan of action.

Plan of Operation

The general plan now employed is for students to go to camp together by classrooms accompanied by their teachers, usually for a period of five school days, as a regular part of their school curriculum. In secondary schools, the camp group may consist of subject matter classes, grades, home rooms, general education units, or special activities that use available camps to achieve general or special objectives of the school program.

The home assumes the cost of food and maintenance, while the board of education provides instructors, materials, equipment, transportation, and special services. Community organizations such as parent-teacher associations and service groups often assist in the initial efforts by way of supplemental financing and other resources.

One of the most significant aspects of school camping is the fact that students and classroom teachers plan the experience cooperatively, go to camp together, and thus relate outdoor learning to the purposes and objectives of their community school. Resource leaders from community, state, and national agencies and organizations are used extensively under the direction of school authorities to enrich the program in these unique "outdoor classrooms." Available camp facilities, public and private, are being leased or rented for this purpose, and in some instances school districts have developed structures in the woods on land controlled by their own or another public agency.

Experience has demonstrated that qualified teaching personnel can do a creditable job of teaching in the camp setting with appropriate in-service training. Those responsible for directing the program are usually chosen because of previous experience and training. The combination of teacher preparation and school camping experience as described elsewhere in this book has been advantageous both to the school camp program and as leadership training.

Program

Program activities in school camping are many and varied. Beginning with basic learning situations involving food, clothing, and shelter, there are unique opportunities for valid experiences in group living, coopera-tive planning, and solving community health problems, not least of which grow from the favorable climate for student-teacher relationships. The outdoor activities within reach are unlimited and can be tailored to the interests and needs of the student and to classroom objectives.

Direct experiences in the outdoors with implications for many school subjects—conservation, health and safety, citizenship, to name a few—make the camp setting a strategic place in which to attain the goals of secondary education. Many outdoor activities possible in the school camping program are described in detail elsewhere in this book.

The use of camps for extended classroom experience is a simple and logical development in curriculum. With careful planning and modest beginnings, it can be initiated without excessive cost or administrative difficulties. With the camp setting as an added resource for the achieve-ment of desired educational goals, the process is simply one of moving into the outdoor laboratory, which constitutes a logical development in general education in a community school.

Work Experiences

One of the great potentials related to outdoor secondary education programs, that may be tied in with the school's camp program either for a setting or as an objective, is in purposeful work experiences on the land. Reminiscent of the CCC, secondary-school leaders should give serious thought to conservation-centered activities that challenge the interests and imaginations of youth while they provide new avenues of learning.

Work-learn camps embodying community service could be designed on the same principles as cooperative programs in vocational education. The Friends Work Camps; Camp Woodland Springs in Dallas, Texas; the Michigan Work-Learning Pilot Program; Camp Paloman, San Diego, California; and others suggest ideas that could be incorporated in *a community school version of the CCC.*[1] Many educators feel that the secondary school could and should provide these kinds of experience for older youth, rather than leave it for other agencies to assume education's responsibility in times of crisis.

Summer Activities

The projection of secondary-school programs into the summer vacation period opens up a whole new area to outdoor education. Already a number of high schools are sponsoring work camps. Farm labor is recruited, transported, supervised, and chaperoned by members of the high-school faculty. In addition to offering an extremely valuable work-ing-earning-saving experience for the high-school youth, a work camp provides for them most of the fine social learnings of any other camp. With adequate safeguards against exploitation, many high schools should move into this area.

There is no good reason why high schools in economically favored areas cannot approximate the open-hearted beneficence so well illustrated by the Quaker Work Camps, where adolescents actually pay to help a war- or disaster-damaged community heal its wounds or to improve community health and recreation in less favored communities. These young-sters pay their own room, board, and transportation and joyfully work to help less fortunate people build, say, a community swimming pool or a playground.

Outdoor Teaching Stations

An outdoor teaching station is one that is particularly rich in opportunities for observing and experiencing real things that contribute to and vitalize certain learning experiences that the teacher or leader is attempting to teach and make meaningful to the group.

These outdoor teaching stations are often the high points of field trips and school camp experiences. They are often the main focus of a trip

---

[1] *A Work-learn Camp for Older Youth* published by Lee M. Thurston, State Dept. of Public Instruction, Lansing, Michigan, 1950.

outside the classroom walls, especially where motor transportation is involved, which is often the case in metropolitan areas.

There are a number of factors to be considered in choosing an outdoor teaching station. It should be close enough to camp or school to make maximum use of time and economical transportation cost. Before a site is chosen, the teacher or leader must have clearly in mind the concepts and knowledge that he wishes to teach or vitalize. The choice is then made of an area that has the most features and elements to help him meet his teaching objectives. The closer together these features are, the more efficient will be his teaching. The safety and the ease with which teaching control can be maintained should also be considered. Once a leader has in mind his objectives for teaching in an outdoor area, he can use the knowledge of resource people to locate possible sites nearby. A county forester, for instance, is usually familiar with the forest areas and can give invaluable leads on sites that would meet the leader's teaching needs.

Once the outdoor teaching station has been selected, the leader must familiarize himself with the area by exploring it for teaching possibilities, using specialists to help him interpret what he is seeing. If he is concerned with natural science and conservation, a good background for the teaching station can be obtained by checking with state agencies concerned with the management of natural areas as it relates to forests, water resources, soil, wild life, *etc.* The leader must then tie this information together as it relates to the specific area and to the grade level of the group with which he is going to work.

Resource People

An outdoor teaching station such as a dam, bird sanctuary, park, forest demonstration area, game farm, or fish hatchery, is usually easier for the leader to develop because his main source of information can often be the person who has charge of the area. However, the leader must still keep in mind his teaching objectives and seek information that will aid him in accomplishing them. If he uses the person who cares for the area to help in the instruction, he should be sure that he has clearly stated his objectives and has been specific in his requests in what he wants the resource person to do and cover. A resource person who has spent his life studying a particular field should not be asked to tell or demonstrate all he knows in the short time that he will be with the group, but he should be given definite questions in the areas of work that will help meet the specific objectives of the outdoor experience the group is having.

Outdoor teaching stations that are chosen to give experience in investigating evidence of man in the past can be of value in vitalizing history, social science, and the changing use of the natural environment by man. These sites are numerous in almost any community—places like abandoned farms, unused roads, farm land reverting to forests, old cemeteries, Indian sites, old quarries, and old water mills. On sites of this type, town histories, old residents, back files of local newspapers, and careful exploration of the site will furnish adequate information for making history and man's way of life in the past come to have vital meaning to the group exploring such an area.

An outdoor teaching station where actual work can be done in the process of discovery or learning is probably the most exciting kind of learning experience from both the standpoint of the leader and the group. Clearing of forest trails, pruning, planting, weeding in a forest, reestablishing foundations by digging, discovery of old bricks, bottles, parts of farm implements, household utensils, and studying their implications are real and vital learning experiences. Using a few of the fundamentals of archeology in exploring and interpreting Indian sites, mounds, *etc.* can contribute to valuable concepts not only of history but also in scientific methods. Care should be taken that sites of this type are checked with the archeologists of the state so that there is no chance that sites of scientific value are disturbed. If the leader is very fortunate, he may be able to have his group do some work under the supervision of a scientist and help make a real contribution to the knowledge of the area.

Outdoor Teaching Methods

A leader must develop good teaching methods if the use of the outdoor teaching station is to be valuable. The lecture approach is probably the least valuable and the one that the leader has the greatest difficulty trying to avoid. A good leader has already acquired a background of knowledge about the area. It is almost irresistible not to tell immediately what he knows to the group. This takes away the thrill of discovery and the need to do any rational thinking on the part of the group.

A good method for an older group is the use of work sheets with leading questions to be answered and the use of guides in the investigation toward the objectives and concepts of the trip. Investigation without intelligent direction from the leader will lead to confusion and wasted time as too many blind alleys will be followed. With younger groups, the question-and-answer method is good. Small groups of four or five can explore and answer two or three questions at a time, coming together with the leader from time to time for evaluation and discussion of the answers and to receive new leads for investigation. Sometimes the objective can be to tell a story which is gradually developed by the group as they investigate the site with each individual contributing to it as they are able.

If the site is historical in nature and historical local knowledge has been studied by the group before the experience, the main activity at the outdoor teaching station can be that of discovering and finding evidence that confirms, or, in some cases, questions the written information studied. It is sometimes exciting to try to confirm stories of old residents about old roads, buildings, caves, cemeteries, *etc.*, that they remember. Some outdoor teaching stations, particularly ones where actual work can be done, are the ones to which you may want to return several times, after periods of study or at different seasons, or after certain things happen such as flood conditions in a flood control area.

If outdoor teaching stations are used properly and are carefully geared to curriculum objectives, they can be a dynamic part of education. Learning requirements for a functioning citizen in our complex civilization are so many that most of them must be vicarious; however, to profit fully from vicarious learning, we must be familiar with some of the direct experience sources from which all knowledge comes. Acquaintanceship in a simple way with the field methods of science, the source materials of historians, and chances to evaluate the things seen, felt, and experienced can give new and more valuable meaning to the information and ideas so conveniently recorded in books and pictured for us through our audiovisual aids to learning.

School-Community Resources

Nature centers, which may be established under the auspices of various agencies, such as schools, museums, and parks, offer secondary-school students unusually fine opportunities for outdoor education. Usually staffed by trained naturalists, with facilities devoted to interpreting the out-of-doors, such centers serve as the focusing point for the nature activities of a community and serve to bridge the gap between the classroom and the out-of-doors.

A nature center generally contains a building used for meetings, lectures, and study. Displays, books, study specimens, laboratory equipment, and nature craft materials may also be included. Some nature centers also have live exhibits, such as reptiles, amphibians, water life, and small mammals. There may also be bird feeding stations that make possible close observation. Equipment for movies and slides are often available.

The building is usually considered a means of interpreting the outdoor area in which it is located, and any displays are directed toward that end. Relief maps, models, charts, and actual specimens give the students a better understanding of the region and relate what they study in the classroom with what they see in the field.

Doorways to Nature

Nature centers may be regarded as doorways to the nature trails that usually radiate from them. An essential feature of the nature center is an outdoor area rich in scientific interest; and nature trails are a valuable means of entering these areas. Such trails make it possible for visiting groups to participate in field trips under the direction of their own teachers or trained leaders from the nature center. In some instances, labeled nature trails, which can be used either without leaders or with leaders unfamiliar with the particular region, have been established.

Nature Center Programs

The Audubon Nature Center of Greenwich, Connecticut, is typical of a number of nature centers. Throughout the school year, both elementary- and secondary-school classes are brought to the center in busses, usually during school time. Teachers come with the groups; and sometimes parents or teachers-in-training augment the supervisory staff. The school groups are met at the center by a member of the center staff, a person trained in the natural sciences and having experience and ability in interpreting to groups the varied outdoor resources of the area. Sometimes class groups may be divided into smaller groups so that more personal attention may be given.

The meeting room of nature centers may be used during bad weather when it is impossible to be out of doors. The center director may conduct lectures and discussions relative to the resources of the area at such times. The meeting rooms may also be used by the teachers for review and evaluation after trips into the field.

Another nature center that has been used heavily by school groups is the Little Red School House operated by the Cook County Forest Preserve District of Illinois. Every attempt is made to make the displays seasonal, and, as a result, the same groups of pupils with their teachers may return several times during a year. The naturalist on duty at the School House explains the exhibits and tells groups how to use the nature trails. The trails themselves are self-guiding; that it, no naturalist need accompany the groups using them. The trails are labeled, and the labels are changed as the seasons progress. The exhibits in the building are local in character and are designed to arouse interest in the vicinity and supply information regarding it. So popular has the Little Red School House become that the Cook County Forest Preserve District is planning other similar centers.

The success of the nature center in contributing to the school program depends upon several things:

Interesting and Varied Approaches to Natural History. The more interesting and varied the area in which the nature center is located, the easier it is to make the program of the center a significant one. Trees, flowers, streams, ponds, birds, animals, insects—all can add to the interest of the center. If, in addition, the geological history and human history of the region are in evidence, the center is rich in program possibilities.

Imaginative, Well-Trained Leadership. Professionally trained leaders, competent in both natural science and educational methods, who can help visiting teachers and pupils, are essential. Such leaders will make the most out of the possibilities of the area.

Concentration on the Local Area. The nature center is not a museum in which may be preserved articles of interest from other parts of the world. It is rather a means of interpreting the living world around it.

Stressing of Basic Principles, Ecological Relationships. By indicating examples of balance in nature, survival, conservation practices, *etc.*, the nature center can demonstrate basic principles which give reality to abstractions studied in the school textbooks and relate classroom work to firsthand experience.

Nature Trails

Nature trails may be established in connection with a nature center or may be set up separately in a park, camp, or school yard. Such trails are designed as outdoor teaching devices and should be located where a variety of natural features may be observed. Trees, flowers, birds, animals, rocks, fossils, water life, and the relationship of living things to their environment are among the things which may be brought to the attention of the trail user.

Trails may be unlabeled or labeled and designed for use either with or without a naturalist guide. Trails which are used under the guidance of a naturalist do not need to be labeled. "Self-guiding" trails, which are intended for use by groups without professional leadership, may have labels placed at numerous points along the trail to interpret the interesting features. Such labels should do more than merely identify; they should, as far as possible, tell a unified story of the area. If trails are not labeled, booklets describing the points of interest may be available for groups to use as they walk over the trails.

Nature trails may vary in length from about a quarter of a mile to several miles. A popular form of trail is one which circles an area, returning the user to a point near that from which he started. Another form of trail is the figure 8, so arranged that users may return to the starting point after covering only half the trail if they so desire.

Available Camps

Camp areas, whether they belong to public or private agencies, may often be employed in the outdoor education program. Since most children's camps operate only in the summer time, they are, as a rule, available to school groups during the school year. Increasingly, schools are obtaining the use of camp facilities both for camping programs during the school year and for one-day trips out of doors.

A good camp site has these desirable features for school groups: an environment in which native plant and animal life is relatively undisturbed; and a varied terrain which makes possible a study of forests, meadows, streams, lakes, and the life therein. In addition, many camps have small museums, nature trails, campfire circles, and other special facilities useful to school groups.

Parks

While school science groups might prefer to work in parks or nature preserves where the native plant and animal life is relatively undisturbed, even the small, well-trimmed city park can be used with profit. Such parks may give the students opportunities to study tree, flower, and bird life and to observe environmental requirements for the continued health of each. The small city park, moreover, offers an excellent opportunity to observe the precautions necessary for the conservation of plant and animal life and the prevention of abuse and damage from over-use. Larger parks may offer a variety of services to school groups, such as museums, nature centers, nature trails, naturalist services, and unusual scientific features.

When a park adjoins the school, the outdoor education possibilities of the school program are greatly enhanced. However, even simple school grounds offer some opportunities. The trees and shrubs around the school and in the near neighborhood are usually sufficient in number and variety to be worthy of study. In some cases, a corner of the school grounds might be reserved for special plantings.

An advantage of school ground science and outdoor education projects, in addition to the ease of observation, lies in the fact that study may take place over various seasons of the year. Another advantage lies in the opportunity to put conservation practices into action and to be able to observe the effect of such action.

Museums

Various kinds of museums may be of service to classroom groups. One is the small museum—set up in connection, perhaps, with a nature center—intended to interpret a local area and containing only exhibits pertaining to that area. Another is the large general museum with comprehensive exhibits from many parts of the world. Some museums are especially designed for children. Other museums are devoted to particular subjects.

Many modern museums are far more than mere centers where objects may be preserved and displayed. They are primarily activity centers, which carry on extensive educational programs, both within the buildings and in the communities in which they are located. Schools fortunate enough to be located near such museums will find many ways in which they can be used: visits to the museums, with professional guidance or with the intention of concentrating on particular subjects; use in the classrooms of materials (films, pictures, specimens, and literature) borrowed from the museums; attendance at lectures in the museums; and participation in special classes or trips sponsored by the museums.

Zoos

There are two main kinds of zoos: large zoos, with animals from all over the world; and local zoos, containing only animals from a limited area. Both kinds may be used by school groups.

Unfortunately most zoos are regarded chiefly as amusement centers. Their educational possibilities are for the large part unexplored. However, they offer an opportunity for students to obtain a firsthand acquaintance with animals and to observe their structure, actions, and habits. Trips through a zoo under expert leadership can be highly instructive.

One means of encouraging purposeful use of zoos is described in *Nature Recreation,* by William Gould Vinal. Each visitor to the zoo is given a sheet of paper (usually mimeographed) containing a number of questions which may be answered either from direct observation of the animals or from information given on labels at the exhibits. Provision

Field trips make learning real.

is made for scoring the answers. Questions such as "How does the tiger differ from a lion?" or "Does the hippopotamus breathe air or water?" encourage observation.

The Special-Project Field Trip

In contrast to the more extended uses of outdoor learning opportunities, there are times when the utilization of very limited amounts of student time for field trips will set in motion chain reactions which permeate and strengthen the conventional program of an entire high school.

The record of this project undertaken by biology classes in a high school serving a medium sized industrial community is cited because it motivated related conservation studies in other school courses. Since biology was a required subject, it involved all students in that grade.

To make biology more real and vital to his pupils, the instructor had set aside time during the fall term to investigate what specific knowledge of biological functions and ecological relationships is required for us to manage intelligently our state's wildlife resources.

Class discussion determined that, for most sections, interest centered upon how to produce better fishing. Specifically, what could be done to increase natural supplies by propagation? What were the minimum environmental requirements for salmonoids? (Apparently the youngsters had been influenced by the thinking of a community rod-and-gun club.)

The instructor then used about two weeks of laboratory study to explore living needs of various fishes in terms of their biological functions. This was linked with class work on microscopic organism (phyto and zooplankton) upon which the fish food chain depends.

A resource person from the fish and game department was invited to come to school for an entire day. Schedules were rearranged to permit all biology pupils to attend a morning assembly, during which a motion picture depicting the propagation of land-locked salmon was shown, and the consultant conducted a general discussion. Subsequently, he met with each biology class in turn to relate these ideas with their laboratory studies.

Biology students expressed eagerness to see for themselves the spawning operation at which fish culturists take eggs from salmon brood stock resident in one of the large lakes, fertilize them on the spot, and transfer them to the hatchery to be reared. Since this required an all-day trip to a distance of about sixty miles, it was deemed impractical to take the entire group. Hence a contest was decided upon.

Selection of Students

Through cooperation with the English department, two essay topics were assigned and the results judged to select about twenty-five boys and girls who would participate:

What is the economic importance of fishing to our state?

What factors are most important to make a lake suitable for salmon?

Parents of selectees cooperated with the instructor to make five cars available for a November visit to the spawning operation. Fish and game department personnel who cooperated with the project included fish culturists, a conservation officer, and the consultant who had visited the school. Students witnessed the taking and fertilizing of eggs. Then they spent more than an hour discussing implications with their resource people. Each school class had designated its spokesmen to secure answers to a prepared list of questions:

Why were the brood salmon kept in the lake?

What did they feed on? How many eggs did each female give? What was the survival rate? Why didn't the state depend upon natural propagation?

What was known about the under-water chemistry and physical factors? What about purity standards? How important were disease problems? What were the mechanics of fertilization; of reproduction?

How much was one adult salmon worth? What did it cost the state? How many fishing licenses were sold each year? Were salmon more valuable than trout; bass? What was the estimated value of tourist business? Where did the fish and game department get money to pay for these operations?

What were the chances of getting a job as a biologist? As a conservation officer? What did one have to know? What should one study in school? What major should one take in college? What college? Were there jobs for girls in conservation?

The field trip group then traveled another ten miles to the hatchery where salmon eggs were being placed on trays to remain until hatched. Students had an opportunity to inspect all facilities of the hatchery and rearing station.

Subsequently, the fish and game department consultant was called back to school for a follow-up visit.

Resource Persons

In the meanwhile the local conservation officer, the sportsmen's club president, and a mill executive had been used as resource people. Now, four months after its inception, the project had taken a new twist. Students were conducting an intensive study of the fishery potential for the river which flowed through their town. While "biology" was still helping, the spring-board was now their social studies classes:

Since this river was tributary to an inter-state giant that flows to the Atlantic, what were the chances of restoring the sea-run salmon that used to frequent its waters?

Whose job was it to control the pollution which their town dumped into the local stream as a result of essential industrial processes?

How important was fishing as compared with other uses of the river? Could you manage to save both?

How many jobs in town depended upon water? Upon other natural resources?

What was the community value of a giant power dam nearby? What was the local responsibility for watershed flood control?

Those are merely indicative of the range of questions which developed from a wildlife conservation problem and led to challenging new school activities. It may be significant that three years later a delegation of seniors from this same school attended the annual meeting of the Connecticut River Watershed Council.

Outdoor Education Through Travel

Travel camping, such as that sponsored a number of years ago by the Atlanta, Georgia, schools, is another fruitful extension of the secondary school into the summer and into the outdoors. Here is the story of how one urban school system fits travel into its learning pattern.

From Canada to the Gulf

From the snows of the Laurentians to the Florida sands, groups of boys and girls from the Roslyn Public Schools in the metropolitan greater New York area have hiked, biked, paddled, skied, and camped in a program that combines adventurous travel, do-it-yourself housekeeping, and group living. No small part of the appeal is in the fact that these modern-day explorers do much of the travel under their own power.

School time, weekends, and holidays are strung together as necessary to permit the number of consecutive days, from three to seventeen, needed for these five to seven yearly trips. Groups are on the road upwards of thirty days a school year.

Trips have been in all directions, with the bicycle the favorite means of transportation. Youngsters have pedaled through New Jersey; various regions of New England; upstate New York, where they visited the capital; out to the tip of Long Island; over by ferry to Shelter Island; through sections of the beautiful Connecticut River Valley; down through Pennsylvania, Maryland, Virginia, Washington, D. C., and as far south as the Gulf coast of Florida. They have also hiked the Horseshoe Trail; canoed in the Adirondacks; skied in Canada, Vermont and New Hampshire; and camped in the jungle and on the beaches of Florida.

It was for a Florida trip that students spent winter weekends designing and building a trailer to transport twelve bicycles and their equipment. Then with camping spots on the Skyline Drive and in state parks, they motored to their base in Florida and explored from it by bike and foot. Because the boys and girls used back roads and trails, the natural beauty that is often hidden by tourist attractions was for the seeing. Here they shared the experience of preparing a jungle meal of wild pig barbecued over the coals of the live oak tree with cooked heart of Palmetto palm. Here too was a natural pool, fringed with palms, whose refreshing water was shared with three alligators. This was high adventure indeed for a group that felt at home in the forest and had dispelled fear with the knowledge that alligators would be content to watch from a distance. There were wild horses in camp; birds, fish, reptiles, and the lush vegetation; camping skills; a look at what is between home and a distant place. But most important, boys and girls had the opportunity to live closely with others and to develop a sense of concern for other people, as well as a feeling of responsibility for their own thoughts and actions. They learned to live with others, by living with others.

How It Began

How did this come about. It started with an interested teacher and a group of students who together wanted to see what was beyond the horizon. They wanted to go slowly enough to see, to feel free to stop and talk with the people they met, to visit places different from their home community, to re-live history at the sites where it was made, to learn, firsthand, what our nation is. At the same time, back in the late 1930's an organization was formed with the purpose of developing healthy, happy, self-reliant, well informed, community and world-minded citizens and providing for inexpensive educational travel opportunities through the development of hostels to be used for overnight stops.

Hostels Provide the Means

The American Youth Hostels, Inc. provides separate bunk rooms and washrooms for boys and girls, a kitchen, and usually a recreation room. Resident house-parents welcome a group as they arrive at the end of a day of "human powered" travel. They may shop nearby, make the evening meal, spend the night, prepare breakfast, clean-up, and be on their way. The facilities are simple, often a converted barn, shop, or part of the farm house. Blankets and cooking pots are furnished. The hostelers carry eating utensils and a sheet sleeping sack.

In this unhurried environment, away from the spectator world into which they were born, boys and girls find a new thrill in active participation. Youngsters today need travel under their own steam. They need to be dependent on their own resources. They need to learn something about the simple life, to get closer to nature and to God. They will be better men and women for it. As youngsters have said, "You learn something on every trip, facts and how to do things. You learn about cooperation, too, and getting along with others. On a trip you decide what to do; in class or at home, someone usually tells you."

Learning Carries Over

How about the academics? Could history be more real than to a group standing on the very spot from which Lincoln spoke his timeless words; or to cyclists looking out over the rolling hills of Valley Forge. Textbook lessons in social studies, English, mathematics, health take on real meaning when we consider meeting new people, planning meals, sharing responsibility, budgeting, building self reliance. The possibilities are endless for direct experiences at a time when they are most meaningful. As a principal has said, "I don't know whether hosteling attracts good students or whether it makes good students, but youngsters with this experience usually do better than average in the classroom."

The group size varies from ten to fifteen on each trip, with one or two teacher-advisers. Because of the big city congestion, most of our trips begin away from Long Island with transportation to the point of departure by train, bus, school bus-station wagon, or private car-bicycle trailer. Except for transportation by public carrier, expenses are no greater than for a day at home. Food and overnights average under two dollars a day.

It was in response to a call for adventure and scientific investigation that led groups of students to make annual underwater diving expeditions to the Florida Keys. There they camp for several weeks on the beaches of uninhabited keys, plan and cook their own meals, trying at times to live off their catch from the sea, and enjoying the thrill of an outdoor group-living experience. The objectives of this trip are varied. They include diving explorations in tropical coral waters, undersea photography, the collection and preservation of marine specimens for our school's science laboratories. Some try their hand at the sport of spearfishing.

Necessity Is a Good Teacher

Much of the equipment necessary for such an expedition is the product of the home work bench. There ingenuity is matched against a student's limited finances. The result has been a remarkable variety of camera cases, diving units re-constructed from old refrigerator parts, "water buckets" with which to view underwater scenes, collection bags, and a variety of guns and spears. While most of the time is spent diving off the coral reefs, there is still an opportunity for sightseeing and visiting with other youth groups. Nor does the activity end with the return to Roslyn. Assembly programs and classroom presentations help to stimulate interest for other trips five-fathoms deep.

Camping as a Human Relations Course

As a result of our favorable experience with transient hosteling as a school activity, we have for seven years included a program that provides many of the values of educational travel with an extended group-living experience in one location. In this program, a class and teachers spend a school week providing for their daily needs and exploring their new environment. A site we use in the Pocono Mountains of Pennsylvania serves as a base for the study of the natural world in a setting of woods, fields, ponds, waterfalls, hills, rocks, and wildlife so scarce in our home community. Another group has lived in a coal mining town and has had the experience of making a community study that included geology, public education and welfare, unions, religions, mines and mining, and young people and their problems. Still another group has lived in a small New England village and participated in its life. Another group has lived in a Pennsylvania-Dutch community.

For many of these experiences, we have drawn upon and used the facilities of the American Youth Hostels which are available to all groups by paying a nominal membership fee. We look forward to having a site of our own in the future, where groups studying the Empire state may find inspiration through participation in outdoor work experiences and conservation effort and may have a feeling of sharing in an on-going educational adventure. This vast, vital educational opportunity is available for all who would but train their eyes to see it, move their legs to achieve it, and open their minds to accept it.

A School Farm Laboratory

Implications for work experience in this school farm are as significant as those for its laboratory use. It is the story of Tyler (Texas) Public Schools' farm laboratory. Covering 180 acres of land, it is probably the largest school laboratory anywhere. It is equipped like a farm, complete with barns, pastures, orchards, implements, silos, farm house, and poultry houses, because it is a farm laboratory maintained by Tyler Schools. It is operated by students who take vocational agriculture in Tyler High School.

Students use the farm in studying agriculture just as they use a biology laboratory in studying biology. When cover crop-planting time comes, two dozen young farmers may be in the field to do the job. If the orchard needs spraying, an entire class will probably take part in the job. If a tractor needs an overhaul, several Future Farmers fall to and do the job in the farm shop.

The seventy-five Future Farmers taking agriculture at the high school are by no means the only youngsters who use the 180-acre laboratory. On almost any school day, a score or more of elementary-school children may be found feeding hens and gathering eggs in the hen house. The next week another class may be getting their farm experience by feeding the pigs. The youngsters visit the farm in the laboratory phase of their outdoor life studies carried on in regular school work.

There is one big difference in this laboratory and, say, a chemistry laboratory. Chemistry laboratories don't pay their own way. The farm laboratory does, because it is operated, as nearly as possible, as a practical farm.

The school farm laboratory has been operating since 1950. Vocational agriculture teachers have nothing but praise for the farm as a laboratory for teaching the best and latest farming methods. The laboratory is a success.

How It Began

Tyler's farm laboratory started with a group of Smith County citizens who became concerned about the lack of outdoor education their children were receiving. Tyler, seat of a county very definitely agricultural, had school children who knew no more about the soil than youngsters growing up on the sidewalks of a huge industrial city. Some children past the first grade in school didn't even know how milk was obtained from a cow. Others didn't know that milk came from cows at all.

This situation resulted in the organization of a group of citizens called the Smith County Youth Foundation. The Foundation set out to see that Tyler youth groups had an opportunity to learn something about the great outdoors and the soil that supports them.

The city of Tyler and the Youth Foundation first cooperated in establishing a 100-acre camp site on the shores of Lake Tyler (twelve miles from town). This camp (named Camp Tyler) was turned over to the school system to be used in regular school for nine months and by various youth groups during the summer vacation.

Just next to this camp property, the Foundation managed to get 180 acres, already partially in a farm, and leased the acreage to Tyler Schools at one dollar a year to be used as a farm laboratory.

Things took shape fast. The vocational agriculture department of the high school was handed the job of operating the farm. Projects began to shape up. Then a local citizen, Judge S. A. Lindsey, gave the ball a rolling push when he donated $15,000 to go toward developing the 180 acres to approximate a typical one-family East Texas farm unit.

Now the vocational agriculture teachers and the Future Farmers could really go to work. The farm landscape acquired a modern Grade A dairy barn and concrete-floored lot, a broiler house, a laying hen house, a remodeled barn, implement sheds, hog lots and feeders, and cattle pens— all painted a neat white and looking like a model farm. Nearly all this work was done by vocational agriculture students.

Since the students can hardly live on the farm day and night, a regular farm manager is hired to look after not only the dairy but also all the enterprises. FFA boys, during regular class periods, work under the farm manager and take instruction from three agriculture instructors on the school staff. The boys do not attend to the milking chores regularly, since they are at home when milking hours come around.

They do, however, keep up with the production records of each cow through a herd book kept by the farm manager and the agriculture instructors. If an instructor wishes to make a point about why a dairy cow should be culled, he can get the book, figure the feed costs against the value of a cow's production, and *show* why she should be culled.

"And if, for instance, we're studying about San Jose scale on fruit trees," says Lawson Sowell, one of the teachers, "we don't have to show a picture or describe how it looks to the boys. We can just take them out in our orchard here to show how it looks, and then how to spray to control it."

The instructors also have the advantage of having good examples of both dairy and beef animals right in their own laboratory as teaching aids. The farm owns more than forty head of dairy animals—Jersey, Guernsey, Holstein, and Brown Swiss—and eight head of Angus beef cattle.

Here in the laboratory, a vocational agriculture student is encouraged to take part in the activity which interests him most. This activity may range from caring for broilers to planting and managing temporary grazing in the pastures.

If a boy has a definite dislike for, say, mechanics, he is not forced to work at repairing the tractor. There are always several lads around who are natural mechanics and would rather tear into the tractor than do anything else.

No matter how a youth spends his time, however, in the classroom, he hears about *all* the operations on the farm. The boys who repaired the tractor tell the entire group what they did and why. The students who cared for the broilers may have to explain why a run of birds failed to show a profit at market time. Others who tended the pigs or the dairy heifers must keep the class posted on progress being made. The idea is to see that a student gets an over-all picture of just what it takes to operate a farm of the type which might make a family a living in East Texas.

Outdoor Education

A regular program of outdoor education is included in the Tyler Public Schools now. Children in the first six grades spend five days at the camp adjacent to the farm, and make visits to the farm laboratory regularly. The director of the school camp says the farm has been the most popular feature of the outdoor education work, as far as the children are concerned. These youngsters in the early grades are not, of course, being taught technical agriculture as the Future Farmers are, but at least they are gaining some basic knowledge of the importance of the soil and the things it produces.

Uses for the farm have been many. High-school biology classes, for instance, visit the farm for field trips; and many groups not even connected with the school system are welcomed at the farm. The artificial dairy breeding association which operates in the county meets at the farm. The first-rate set of pastures developed on the place has furnished interesting material for pasture tours of farmers and ranchers of Smith County. Many groups and individuals representing the various farm agencies have used the farm laboratory for meetings or demonstrations.

No, the farm laboratory does not make a lot of money. However, it is self-sustaining, a characteristic any school official loves about a school facility. But the very fact that so many youngsters use the farm laboratory reduces its chances of showing big profits. When second-grade pupils gather eggs, for instance, they're bound to break some and are likely to frighten the hens and discourage production a bit. These things cut into profits. Any farmer knows that his income is not going to be increased by allowing every citizen in the country to roam over his farm; particularly, if the farmer encourages the visitor to take a sample of everything he sees. This, in effect, is what happens at the farm laboratory, because it is part of the laboratory's function.

When milk or eggs or broilers or any other product of the farm is sold, the money goes into the general school fund. At the same time, if supplies at the farm are needed, they are bought with money from the same fund. However, a separate financial record for the farm is kept so that school authorities know at any time how the laboratory is going, money-wise.

So far, it has been going nicely, and at this stage the laboratory is no longer in an experimental stage. It is an accepted part of the school system and is doing the job which the Smith County Youth Foundation, several years ago, dreamed that it would. And in a few years it should be impossible to find an elementary-school child in Tyler who believes—as one once did—that the dairyman gets milk by pressing on the sides of a cow.

School Forests

For many schools throughout the country a school forest constitutes a natural outdoor education center. In other instances, municipal, county, state, and national forests can be used similarly by schools. Most of the descriptions of outdoor educational activities would be appropriate in the use of forest lands that are available to schools.

The idea of school forests largely grew out of the period when the needs for reforestation were beginning to be evident. A consciousness about the fate of the cut-over lands where great forests had been, and the development of a concept of proper land use impelled agriculture and conservation leaders to educate the public about the need for conservation and wise use of natural resources. Farming had followed the great timber slash with little or no attention to the ability of the land to raise farm crops. Often a bare existence for those who moved out on the lands followed and, finally, a reversion of the properties to the state government due to tax delinquence resulted. It was during this period that the practice of deeding land to counties, townships, cities, villages, and schools developed. While the original purpose was to get the land replanted to trees and demonstrate the need for better reforestation and land use, it was hoped by many that the forests would help serve the educational and recreational needs of the communities, particularly the schools.

Legislation was enacted in several states, permitting the establishment of county, township, village, city, and school district forests. In most instances the properties were deeded by the state agency holding the lands, such as the department of conservation with provisions that reforestation and timber management practices be carried out.

In 1927 a law was enacted in Wisconsin and revised in 1949 which reads as follows: "Sec. 28.20. Any city, village, town, or school district may acquire land, engage in forestry, and appropriate funds for such purposes. In the case of a city or village or school forest, the forest property may be located outside the city or village limits."

As a result of such laws, many hundreds of parcels of land varying in size from a few acres to several hundred were deeded to Michigan schools. In districts where there were high schools, the agriculture department usually took the lead in carrying out the reforestation program. Trees were furnished by the state department of conservation, and most of the land was soon planted to trees which were appropriate to the soil and location.

During the time of low-priced land and available tax-reverted tracts, many schools purchased land for forest purposes. Like the others, the major part of the earlier use was for tree planting, but, in many instances, far-sighted administrators and teachers saw in the school forest new opportunities for outdoor education, related to the school's instructional program.

Purposes of the School Forest

The school forest has two major purposes: (1) through reforestation and management of the plot, to develop an understanding of the growth and wise use of the forest; and (2) to provide an outdoor laboratory for learning activities that can take place best in a forest environment.

Forestation and Management

The first of these purposes is concerned primarily in getting proper land use of the specific piece of land and to develop public concepts and attitudes about good conservation practices. It also demonstrates the social and economic benefits accruing from proper land use, develops an appreciation of the importance of woodlands, and encourages those who own property to carry out good woodland management. If the school forest was made possible by a land grant, the school had specific responsibilities in carrying out the original purposes. Periodic reporting is necessary and there should be working relationships with local, state, and national units of government in achieving the greatest results and providing channels for interpretation to the public.

A sample form for reporting is suggested in a publication on *School Forests* by Michigan State University.[2]

The development of the school forest to satisfy the purposes of the land grant requires careful and somewhat technical management. Some of the activities included may be:

1. Mapping and establishing boundary lines
2. Making a master plan
3. Tree planting
   a. Areas to plant
   b. Choice of stock and obtaining trees
   c. Ground preparation
   d. How to plant
4. Care of plantations
5. Christmas tree production
6. Tree protection and disease and insect control
7. Thinning and pruning
8. Harvesting
   a. Marking and scaling
   b. Sale

---

[2] *School Forests—Their Educational Use,* Cooperative Extension Service, Michigan State University, East Lansing, Michigan.

All of these activities can be of great value to the adult participants and all those that may observe the process over the years. As one would expect, it is sometimes difficult for a community to keep a substantial interest in the program over a period of years unless there is constant use of the forest for school and community activities. More effort and planning is required for the less spectacular process of management.

General Educational Use of the Forest

The use of the school forest in the educational program of the community school is almost unlimited. There is an increasing trend for school districts to purchase parcels of land often located near the central school buildings that can be developed into forests. In many communities there are pieces of marginal lands often barren and un-sightly that could be purchased reasonably. In some cases, pieces of land are given to schools by private individuals or industries. Sometimes these areas are wooded and well developed, and, in other instances, the site may be an abandoned farm or deserted real estate subdivision. In either situation, there is a great opportunity for a unique educational program which will pay big dividends in community education and often with some financial profit.

Witness, for example, some of the beautiful pines now growing on what were denuded and eroded hillsides that were planted in the late thirties or early forties by the CCC. In some sections of the country roadside signs will be seen pointing to a school forest or a public recreation area which was once a barren and unused piece of land.

One of the greatest values of a school forest might accrue in the selection, purchase, planning, and development of the site. The permanent values to youth in having had a part in the development of land may well be the school's greatest contribution to citizenship and social responsibility. Many state and local subdivisions now have maps and aerial photographs and descriptive material of lands. Whether a school obtains its forest from public authorities or purchases it from private owners, the project should be a whole school affair as much as possible. In contemplating such an event, school-community planning committees should be formed. Many resources are available for help, such as the county agricultural agent; the soil conservation service; national, regional, and state forest offices; conservation and parks de-partments; colleges; and others. Much literature is available such as the school forestry publications, conservation department materials, and others.

School Forest Programs

Many outdoor education activities in other kinds of situations such as parks, camps, and farms are available in the school forest. Forests usually are the habitat of more wild animals and birds than would normally be found in a small and more domesticated area near the

An outing club high in the White Mountains of New Hampshire.

school. Obviously, there are also more opportunities to study trees and observe the interrelationships that exist among plants, animals, soil, and water.

Some of the more common uses of the forest for instructional purposes include:

1. A laboratory for elementary classroom activities, such as science, social studies, music, art, and conservation.

2. Learning opportunities for school groups with special interests, such as forestry, agriculture, conservation, botany and zoology, history, shop, and raising Christmas trees.

3. Opportunities for development of skills and hobbies, such as use of native materials, simple shelter construction, fire protection, archery, and camp crafts.

4. An outpost facility where camp shelters may be constructed for day or resident camping.

5. A recreation resource for the community for picnics, hikes, and other outdoor activities appropriate to the environment and to the property.

Outing Clubs

School clubs offer many opportunities for outdoor activities, particularly in secondary schools. An increasing number of schools now regard the club program as a part of the curriculum offerings and provide adequate leadership and time to make them worth while. With such activities organized each year on an interest basis, the club program can become vital in enriching the school's entire instructional program. A great variety of outdoor clubs will be formed in schools. Some of the types reported include: outing, conservation, fishing, hunting, skiing, bait casting, riflery, fly tying, fly casting, taxidermy, hiking, birds, canoeing, outdoor science, forestry.

Outdoor clubs are usually organized so that some time can be spent during the regular period provided in the school for discussion, study, business of, and planning for field experiences. Often the most interesting and valuable parts of the club are the trips, camp outs, and other informal activities that are planned by the participants. Some examples of different kinds of clubs, illustrating how they can become an important part of the curriculum, are described below.

Mountaineering and Camping Clubs

Having taught for many years in high school, I know how crowded the program has become. Climbing, camping, and skiing are handled in many high schools through extracurricular organizations.

Here at West High School in Bremerton (Washington), they are a part of the intramural program. All the students interested in outdoor activities are invited to join the Outdoor Club. Banded together, they plan a number of activities for the year. Objectives and the organization of the club are reconsidered each year by the students themselves before the program is laid out. In the fall, the club enjoys fishing, hiking, and camping. In the winter, they ski. Again in the spring, they hike and climb. Before their trips, each group meets to go over the important factors to be kept in mind—what to observe on the trip, and safety measures. Before ski season, there is a short ski school under the direction of a leading skier of this area who presents three evening lectures. Advanced skiers are present on ski slopes to help beginners learn properly. This popular club is filling a real need for students of outdoor activities in our high school.

Cooperative Curriculum Planning

Living, as we do, on the Olympic Peninsula, in the very shadows of the Olympic mountains, it is natural for young people and adults of this area to turn to the mountains for recreation. Our location is the chief reason that Olympic College and the cooperating high school have developed outdoor classes as part of their regular curricula. From our experience, we can say that teaching outdoor education through family camping, summer hiking and camping classes, climbing, and skiing is a worthy addition to the program of schools interested in teenagers.

The thought of climbing, camping, and skiing, as classes, is new and was developed here only after careful planning by a committee composed of high-school instructors and interested citizens who met with the administrators of Olympic College (a junior college, also in the town of Bremerton, Washington). It was decided to offer a class in climbing. The committee felt that it would be better to offer the class as a part of the evening-school program so it could be available to the entire community.

Mountaineering

Basic training in mountaineering is just as essential as training in major sports. Any program that requires personal skill and a degree of calculated risk demands a training program before students should be encouraged to undertake it.

The Seattle Mountaineers were well known for the classes that they conducted for their members. They accepted our request for help, and soon a curriculum was planned and a class scheduled. We then sent special invitations to all high-school students in our county to join the class if they liked to climb. There was immediate response, and classes have been held every spring for the past seven years. Scarcely a student in this area who likes to climb fails to enroll.

Lectures are given in the evening, and the field trips and climbs are on weekends. The following is a sample schedule:

LECTURES	FIELD TRIPS
Mar. 22—Registration and orientation; exhibition of equipment	Mar. 24 or 25—Green Mountain (orientation)
Mar. 29—Basic rock climbing and rope fundamentals	Apr. 7 or 8 —Monitor Rock (rock climbing practice)
	Apr. 21 or 22—Little Si (rock practice)
Apr. 5—Safety	Apr. 28 - 29 —Cayuse Pass (snow practice)

LECTURES	*CLIMBS*
Apr. 12—First aid	May 12 or 13—Mt. Ellinor
Apr. 19—Trail techniques and camp cooking	May 19 or 20—Mt. Baldy
	May 26 - 27 —The Brothers
Apr. 26—Basic snow climbing	June 2 or 3 —Mt. Washington
May 3—Final examination	June 10 —Glacier practice on Mt. Rainier

Climbing is taught and conducted as a regular class and requires completion of work. Members must pass a written test on lectures, take three out of four field trips, and achieve two climbs at least. The interest in this program and the need it fills is shown by the fact that most of the students do much more than the required work.

While our location is only two hours drive from a mountain range, we start our practice in the high-school gymnasium. Access to an irregular wall or bulkhead can serve to teach techniques in finger and toe holds and rock climbing. Many of our students practice extra time at a rock quarry nearby. It is convenient for us to use the facilities of the Olympic Community College for our classes, but any high school could successfully organize this type of program.

For the young mountaineer, climbing fills his waking hours from morning until night. Though he may not realize it, he is attracted to study and read everything on the subject of mountains; he clamors for information. Soon he can readily name the great climbers of history and the heights of the highest peaks; and he learns about the terrific hardships climbers overcome to reach the top of each peak. The program opens a new avenue for comradeship. Climbing does not attract the lazy.

Meeting Living Needs

The question is often asked, "Why do those kids want to climb? What is this attraction to the mountains?" There is a call, an appeal to climbing for young people that many adults find hard to understand. The fact is that boys and girls enjoy and seek a chance to test themselves; they want to pit their strength against odds; they have to show their friends that they are grown up.

A generation ago a great percentage of the "teens" were needed on the farm and in family work. They had responsibilities. What is there in the modern home to challenge the physically growing boy or girl? Rapid physical development gives our youth a surplus of energy. Apart from the physical challenge, climbing is a mental and spiritual challenge. Also, the mountain is something real. The climber wants to climb a mountain because "it is there." Climbers see their mountain, move toward it as an objective. The biting wind whips them in the face. They must push on though they are weary; they develop self-control. The climber must refrain from looking down the deep crevasse or vertical wall. He must conquer the fear of "height that grips." When he reaches the summit, he can sit on top and look around at the lower peaks. He sees progress and he thrills at conquest; he realizes satisfaction because he has accomplished an objective.

The difficulty is really not the point. He endures heat or extreme cold, the obstruction of snow, dizzy heights, obscure routes, jagged rock, fatique —nothing stops him but the top of the peak; he has made the top! Climbers realize risks, but they overcome them. On the way down, they can look back on the peak where they sat a short time before. They can point out that peak to their friends. "We were on that top rock at two o'clock last Saturday afternoon," they brag; and the thrill is lasting.

Nor are the rewards all stern and severe. In the summer, there is the warm sun, the mountain meadows filled with flowers, the rushing streams, the murmur of waterfalls, the welcome rest in the shade, the refreshing drink of water, the delicious fragrance of the clean, fresh air, and the sight of bear, deer, and marmots. Near the peaks, the climber enjoys the brilliant blue color in the glacial ice and the sparkling snow. Always there is the joy of comradeship and the appeals that make lasting impressions on the young climber.

Considering this enthusiasm and determination, these students must have training to be safe in the mountains. Training, given in classes as we give it, is a part of the physical education schedule. It can be part of the intramural program or a project of organized clubs. One fact is clear: some type of training is necessary.

Camping

The summer period is an excellent time for training in camping. For a number of years, we have offered successful camping classes using the same school advisers that met with the climbing classes. Membership in our summer camping and pack-trip classes is open to a wide scope of ages. Since many of our members are teenagers, we again work with the high schools.

One class in campcraft completes a fifty-mile trek through the most primitive and scenic part of the Olympic National Park. Another class stays at a base camp in the Olympic Mountains for two weeks of instruction in art and campcraft, with a minimum of hiking to suit those unable to endure rigorous climbing. Both classes are offered during a July-August period and are part of the regular summer-school schedule.

Each day the classes enjoy some type of camping instruction from accredited teachers in a variety of subjects including Alpine flowers, plants, and animals of the National Park, weather, climate, geology, astronomy, photography, first aid, camp cooking, basic campcraft, safety, hiking, climbing, and the art of group living.

While the trips are carefully planned ahead of time in every respect, ample opportunity is given to participating members to plan fun at the campfires, to choose side trips, and to enjoy their experiences of living together. Everyone in the mixed group shares in the camp work through rotating committees as aids in better acquaintance.

3. Enrich Living Through Outdoor Experiences

THREE factors in modern life have tremendously influenced the participation in outdoor activities. These are increased leisure, increased income, and increased mobility. With more time and more money at their disposal and with better roads and more automobiles than ever before, Americans are able to get out of doors in unprecedented numbers.

The extent of the participation of the American public in outdoor activities each year is indicated by statistics which show that there are 54 million visitors to the national parks each year, 40 million users of the national forests, 183 million who visit state parks, 21 million fishermen, and 11 million hunters. More that 12 billion dollars are spent annually in the travel and vacation business.

The movement of city dwellers to the suburbs has created a new group in American society, a group whose work is tied to the city, but whose living is semi-rural and whose leisure interests lie largely in the out-of-doors. Outdoor-related hobbies have risen to new heights of popularity. Bird-watchers, "rockhounds" who collect and polish rocks, amateur archeologists, botanists, and astronomers are legion in number. The forests and parks are filled with campers, hikers, and boating enthusiasts —all seeking satisfaction in the out-of-doors.

This great exodus has not come without creating problems. Sometimes the pressure of numbers takes from the outdoor areas the very thing that the visitors seek. Highways are crowded, parks and forests are inadequate, camp grounds are congested, fishing streams are seriously overused. Manifold problems arise with overuse and misuse: litter on highways and in parks and forests, the defacement of natural features, the destruction of plants, the flouting of game laws, the indiscriminate killing of non-game animals, the erosion of soil tramped upon by too many feet, the destruction of signs and labels, fires resulting from carelessness, and damage to facilities and equipment because of vandalism. Outdoor accidents—most of them preventable—are far too prevalent.

What is the school's responsibility in outdoor usage? If our outdoor resources are to serve future generations, the school can make a major contribution in teaching young people to regard their outdoor heritage with respect, to cherish and protect resources in danger of serious depletion, and to restore and repair damage wherever possible. The school can give instruction in accident prevention out-of-doors and in outdoor good manners—lessons which in many cases can be taught only in the outdoor setting itself.

A second major contribution that the school can make in outdoor usage is concerned with the development of skills and interests for the worthy use of leisure time. The American people today turn in ever-increasing numbers to outdoor pursuits for satisfactions that are deep and enduring. Those who attain such satisfaction will inevitably be concerned with the conservation of our natural resources for generations to come.

The following descriptions present a few of the many outdoor experiences that are logically a part of the secondary-school curriculum and have tremendous life enrichment value.

Campcraft and Outdoor Living

From deep within us all there are urges that can be satisfied only through an experience in the out-of-doors. People generally need an exposure to the elements—through elemental experiences. They need to have contact with forest and field, snow and smoke, wind and water. Their lives will be richer for having had an opportunity to acquire new physical skills and mental attitudes and to live in the out-of-doors, in the woods, on a lake, up a mountain. Three elemental experiences come quickly to mind—with shelter, with fire, and with food.

Shelter

In regard to shelter, most people can remember the fun that they got out of throwing a blanket over a line in the backyard and calling it a tent, or of finding a packing case to play in, or the very real pleasure of crawling inside a cardboard box and sitting out in the rain looking out and feeling comfortable and protected. This must be closely related to the sense of security that our ancestors got as they crawled into their caves and looked out at the elements pouring down about them.

There is a fascination with fire—man, for example, doesn't just burn leaves in the fall to get rid of the leaves, but because there is a fascination about the fire. Children will build fires in vacant lots and play about them, sit and talk. The fascination of a fireplace is carried over even today into our most modern architectural forms where we don't really need the fire for warmth, but use it as a symbol of our heritage.

Food Preparation

Food preparation presents a particular kind of fascination for all people, not only because of the creative expressions that are possible, but also because it is such a satisfying occupation! The proverbial hot dog on a skewer isn't a difficult culinary task, but the inward feeling of accomplishment might be akin to that of primitive man with his raw meat on a stick.

Through quite a variety of youth-serving agencies, boys and girls are getting an opportunity to participate in programs of campcraft and outdoor living. But it isn't enough to acquire some of these skills at an early age and then never use and develop them further. These competencies need to be practiced and constantly improved for successful living in the out-of-doors.

Campcraft Skills

Skills that form a backlog for campcraft can include the following: toolcraft, knotcraft, firecraft, cooking, map and compass, equipment and gear, safety and sanitation, conservation.

With tools, a person should be familiar with the utilization of woods tools. He should be able to handle a knife, axe, and saw with sufficient knowledge to do the cutting that is necessary without harm to himself and others. He should know the proper care of these tools—how to sharpen, store, and repair them. More stress is being placed in camps today on the utilization of saws rather than axes for many cutting purposes—it is a much safer tool and one that can accomplish the necessary work in short order.

In knotcraft, a person should be able to know and properly use three or four of the common knots (square, clove hitch, bowline, timber hitch), and he should also be able to do some lashing for general campcraft construction work. With firecraft, a person should be able to make a careful selection and preparation of the fire site and the proper selection of materials for tinder, kindling, and fuel. He should also be able to construct three different types of fires and demonstrate the proper extinguishing of fires.

Skills a camper should have in the cooking area would include such things as being able to plan, prepare, and pack a couple of different style meals. He should be able to set up a camp kitchen and demonstrate proper sanitation and cleanup techniques. Simple one-pot meals are good for beginnings and the outdoor chef can move on to more complicated cooking and reflector baking as he gains in experience.

Knowing where to go and how to come back depend on a person's ability to use map and compass. In addition to these aids, a person should be able to find his direction by sun and stars and should be able to orient himself in the out-of-doors. The utilization of the Silva compass is covered in the section headed "Orienteering" found near the end of this chapter.

In regard to equipment and gear, campcrafters need to gain skills in selecting, packing, and carrying personal clothing and program and safety items for personal and group use. This should include such things as packs, shelter (tents, tarps, *etc.*) tools, sleeping bags, sports equipment, first aid kits, *etc.*

Safety and sanitation procedures are necessary throughout any kind of campcraft and outdoor living program. Provision should be made for utilizing proper procedures with tools, knots, fires, cooking, *etc.* In addition, persons engaged in campcraft should know and realize their limits as far as adequate rest, balanced food, and protection from hazards is concerned. This necessitates competent leadership and careful planning throughout.

Wise Use of Natural Resources

All campcraft and outdoor living activities should be permeated with consideration of the wise and careful use of the natural resources that surround us. Finding the natural resources that are available and using them wisely is a part of conservation education. Campcrafters should be vitally concerned with the replacement and improvement of areas utilized and should be concerned with the necessity for careful cleanup and the following of good manners in the out-of-doors. These skills are not meant to be mutually exclusive—they are a vital part of any good experience in campcraft and outdoor, and they should serve as a guide to persons setting up the program of work for people to be thus involved.

If we can assist people to find the satisfactions that come through the acquisition of skills and the development of a friendly familiarity with the out-of-doors, we will be doing much towards contributing to their welfare. Giving them an opportunity through participation in activities of this sort on an individual, family, and group basis and placing this kind of experience in God's green out-of-doors are significant events in the lives of people. Giving them an opportunity to wonder and to wander and find their place in the physical universe is a challenge too great to be skimmed over lightly.

When a program of this sort is introduced into a school setting at the high-school level, it would be in order to recognize the fact that some of the persons to be involved may have had an exposure to it with youth groups. Less than fifteen per cent of our total child population receive an organized camp experience, however. The teenager, especially, needs the opportunity to engage in campcraft and outdoor living experiences. The program will need to be geared to an intensive level, however, to hold him. Intensity does not necessarily mean more complicated or involved—the writer feels that it may also mean the development and encouragement of simplicity, of "getting back to fundamentals." The teenager ought to feel the challenge of work, of taking his full share, of following through on responsibilities, of seeing the relationship of his endeavors to those of others. In a camping program, they can sense the "oneness," the consciousness of the group, and they can recognize the importance of working cooperatively in a relaxed, uncomplicated setting away from the gadgets of ordinary life. They need mature, trained leadership who can assist them in decision-making, in developing and strengthening their inner resources, and in guiding their way to fuller independence.

Through the organization of such groups as camping clubs, outing clubs, ski clubs, etc., it would be possible to carry on a vital program of campcraft and outdoor living. Regular meetings of the group with skill sessions, opportunities for members to teach others, sharing experiences, making equipment, planning-organizing-carrying out and evaluating a variety of outdoor experiences are invaluable learnings.

The following was written as a description of a collegiate outing club which the writer once directed. It has much in common with the program that can be developed on the high-school level. It is entitled, "This Is Us".

We . . . are commonly known as a pretty odd group of people . . . who climb mountains because we like the view from the top . . . who go out hiking because . . . well . . . because we like the sun on our backs or the rain on our ponchos. . . . When night comes we square dance or sit around the campfire singing the old songs that campfire squatters have sung always . . . loving the sight of fire-light on the faces of our friends. . . . We don't happen to drink on our trips because liquor seems to be an unnecessary commodity . . . and besides . . . who wouldn't be "half-seas over" at the mere sight of a friend hanging from a rafter . . . safely zipped in a sleeping bag. . . . We boast the weirdest hats in the nation . . . faster fire builders than the Boy Scouts . . . though perhaps not with a single match . . . and undoubtedly the most perverted sense of humor since Joe Miller let loose his humor on the unsuspecting multitudes. . . . We don't tend to couple on our trips because . . . we like the give and take (as in food) of a group . . . and we like to carry the idea of . . . individuality within a group . . . into all phases of our program . . . and even into our personal philosophy . . . many people think we're crazy . . . we are sure of it. . . . We haven't written this to edify ourselves . . . we know it at heart. . . . This is for you who might want to know us better . . . like this page . . . we lack much formal organization . . . but still . . . this is us.

—SANDY ROSEBROOK
Syracuse University Outing Club

A State Program for Shooting Education

A primary objective of outdoor education is providing skills for lifetime enjoyment. Shooting can be classified as one of the activities that old and young, male or female, and even the physically handicapped can enjoy. While the immediate goal of the program reported here was positive skill training and the acquiring of firearms knowledge as a means of accident prevention, promotion of an activity in the public schools that would open new avenues in outdoor education was envisioned as an important outcome.

Before this program of firearms safety and training for shooters had been underway in New Hampshire for two years, eighty-two per cent of the state's high schools had introduced aspects of it in their curricula. Community readiness probably contributed most to local program initiation. In addition, a permissive statute was enacted by the state legislature. This law authorized any school district, which so wished, to teach safe handling of firearms, and to appropriate money for this purpose.

Building upon previous skeleton programs prepared by the National Rifle Association and materials furnished by Sporting Arms and Ammunition Manufacturers' Institute (SAAMI), three departments within the state government worked cooperatively to provide material for a course of study and to give assistance in the implementation of the program—education, fish and game, and the state police. The last two departments were interested because it was their personnel who were usually associated with the tragedy of a firearms accident. They realized that an eventual drop in gun-accident casualty statistics would be fundamentally a matter of education.

Conservation officers cooperate with the school in teaching the safe use of firearms.

It was made clear from the outset that each school should provide instructors from its own staff. The program administration and instruction should be teacher-centered. Fortunately, concrete evidence was available to prove the fact that skill training would be effective in reducing accidents—from the five-year record achieved by the National Rifle Association's young trainees in New York state, and from results attained through driver education programs in New Hampshire schools, which had reduced automobile casualties among trained students by at least fifty per cent.

Before the school program was available, it was necessary to establish basic concepts, provide a course of study containing material which was not a matter of the printed word, train teachers for the program, and provide access to competent consultants. School personnel must realize that the need applies to entire school populations, not just potential hunters. Statistics for New Hampshire, as well as for the entire nation, indicate that the majority of gunfire accidents occur outside the hunting field, and that juveniles are involved in more than their share.

A planning committee of specialists from education, conservation, state police, SAAMI, the National Rifle Association, and rod and gun clubs was assembled. Worth-while programs depend upon some standardization of instruction—especially in the area of safety education. The logical approach for such information seemed to be from men who had firsthand knowledge of New Hampshire's actual problems in the field.

A clinic was organized and administered to the entire force of conservation officers in the state fish and game department and members of the state police. Competent lecturers and discussion leaders spearheaded this first effort. The officers served as an exploratory group, contributed their practical knowledge, and, at the same time, were trained to act as consultants to the schools in their districts. The Governor of New Hampshire, the fish and game director, the superintendent of the state police, the commissioner of education, and the executive director of the National Rifle Association, all participated in the clinic. In this first effort, the elements of a practical program of firearms safety education were established. The entire clinic was tape recorded, and the proceedings were made available for future use in constructing a course of study. A second clinic was sponsored for teachers of the program and faculty members from interested schools. Eighty-four per cent of New Hampshire's school unions participated, along with superintendents and principals.

Instructor's Guide

As a result of these two clinics, a group of high-school instructors, reinforced with competent consultants, had been trained for a state-wide program of firearms education. The joint insight and experience of educators, law enforcement personnel, representatives from the arms and ammunition industry, and the National Rifle Association were now on record. The tape recording of the clinics and available literature were transformed into an *Instructors' Guide*. The subject matter was organized into logical teaching units. The *Guide* contains practical information concerning organization and administration of the program, program materials, audio-visual aids, method of teaching, testing procedures, pre-testing; general knowledge of guns, rifles, shotguns, and pistols and pre-testing; general knowledge of guns, rifles, shotguns, and pistols, and ammunition; proper and safe handling of guns; instruction and demonstration range procedure and class firing; hunter's responsibility and parents' responsibility, lost hunter and non-hunter; accidents; field trips; and evaluation. Many teachers have utilized the entire program in their specific areas of instruction or taught certain units through course integration.[3]

As a result of administrator and teacher evaluation, the program received high approval, not only by school personnel, but also by parents and the participating students. Instructional level was judged most effective for grades eight, nine, and ten.

Films

In addition to the *Instructors' Guide,* the fish and game department produced two excellent sound-color films which may be obtained on a rental basis. The first, *Death Is a Careless Hunter,* is dramatic shock treatment. It re-enacts a deer-hunting fatality which actually took place in the New Hampshire woods a few years ago and the subsequent law enforcement routine and emotional impact on the man who did the shooting.

The second film, *Tomorrow We Hunt,* is the story of a teenage boy who, wanting to handle his gun and to hunt, used the New Hampshire Plan to persuade his dad and the school authorities to make firearms training available. This film is an attempt to describe the evolution of one state's program.

It should be emphasized that the success of the program was realized through the splendid co-operation of the state department of education, fish and game, and state police; local rifle and sporting clubs; local school personnel; Winchester Repeating Arms; Remington Arms; Sporting Arms and Ammunition Manufacturers' Institute; and the National Rifle Association.

A School Program for Hunting

With shorter working hours and longer weekends, people are turning to the out-of-doors in ever increasing numbers which means that there are more hunters roaming the woodlands—hunters who can be a hazard if ignorant and careless, or who may be trained in the skills of hunting and gun safety and taught the aesthetic values that mother nature has to offer.

It has been pointed out by the National Rifle Association that 2,500 people are killed each year by gunshot. Strangely enough 1,000 such accidents occur in the home, and of these 90 are children under four years

---

[3] This guide is the prototype of the Guide issued by the American Association for Health, Physical Education, and Recreation.

of age. This would appear to point to a lack of training of adult and young alike in the use of firearms.

About the richest heritage a man could leave to this world would be an educated family—educated not only in the sense of achieving a high standard of living, but also in the sense of enriched recreation. As teachers we have been taught that one of the cardinal principles of education is *the worthy use of leisure time.* If we sincerely believe this, it should justify including hunting as a sport on the same level as baseball, football, basketball, or any other activity that is given a portion of time in any high-school curriculum.

Objectives of such a hunting-shooting clinic or program in secondary education might include the following:

1. To develop reliability and independence
2. To develop self-discipline and sportsmanship
3. To teach proper and safe method of handling firearms
4. To develop an appreciation of the out-of-doors
5. To develop an understanding of the state game laws and the reasons for enforcement

Fitting Hunting Into the Program

These objectives may be carried out in various ways. Some schools may integrate their materials in special classes such as biology, science, or conservation. An ideal situation would be an integrated program on hunter-safety training, involving all subjects; *i.e.,* history, art, English, homemaking, and the rest. However, school staff cooperation is necessary to make the program successful.

An Extracurricular Activity

Most schools today set aside a portion of the day for extracurricular activities. It is during this time that a worth-while program on hunting and shooting could be put into effect whereby everyone can be reached. To be really effective the program should be made available for all first-year hunters and to other interested students.

In order to obtain full cooperation, the parents and the community should be made aware of the program offered by the school by means of a letter to parents and by newspaper publicity, outlining the objectives of the course and indicating what is to be taught and by whom. If there is to be excused time from school for hunting, the parents should be told what standards must be attained by the student before he would be given released time.

Some of the basic areas included in the hunting-shooting education program at Graveraet High School in Marquette, Michigan, are:

1. *State Game Laws.* A lecture-discussion by qualified instructors on the current hunting laws in effect, with special emphasis on the interpretation to young hunters 18 years old and less. Materials are available from many sources, some of which are listed in the bibliography.

Fishing is enjoyed by young and old.

2. *Small Game Management.* A lecture-question or discussion session that deals briefly with rabbit, grouse, squirrel, and migratory fowl. This includes their habitat, customs, food desired, and their general availability in the vicinity.

3. *Management of Deer and Bear.* This session covers the habitat, food, cover, and customs of the large game animals. It discusses summer and winter habitat, the dangers involved in hunting these species, and the regions which they are likely to frequent.

4. *Gun Safety and Proper Clothing.* This session should be considered as one of the most important meetings of the class. It should be presented by qualified instructors with help from the class and should include all types of guns, their care and condition, as well as proper handling. Different members of the group could demonstrate the proper clothes to wear.

5. *Compass Reading and Map Orientation.* This session includes the proper reading of a compass and elementary map reading. Maps of the students' own locality should be distributed, and tips on how to use the maps would be in order. Part of the session could be devoted to "What to do and not to do when you are lost."

6. *Fire Prevention.* This session can be devoted to fires of all types—how they start, how they act, and the damage that can result. Emphasis should be placed on the careless camper and the careless smoker. Materials are available from many sources.

7. *First Aid.* This session can be an excellent one if presented by a local doctor who is an ardent hunter. Elementary first aid, such as the treating of shock, tourniquets, artificial respiration, and emergency carries, should be discussed and demonstrated.

8. *Law Enforcement.* This field could be covered by enforcement agency personnel. Laws and cases that have any bearing on hunting could be discussed at length. Procedure in locating lost hunters and other related fields should be described.

9. *Gun Care.* This session should be presented by the local resource leaders and should point out the different types of guns and ammunition. The importance of proper cleaning and storage should be stressed.

10. *How To Dress and Care for Your Game.* This session can be presented by a local butcher who would do an excellent job on this subject. Charts and other illustrations can be used to supplement the discussion. Recipes that deal with wild game could be discussed and materials, containing such recipes, could be distributed.

It would be well, if excused time is given for hunting, that students present evidence of adequate training in firearms safety. Each student meeting the standards should then present his hunting license and a statement of approval written by his parents to the proper school authorities prior to the released hunting time. (The length of time will vary according to the locality and type of hunting.)

The above type of program should give the student a new insight to our outdoor world. It will make him not only a more efficient hunter but also a better sportsman in a world where good sportsmanship is lacking many times. With this better understanding will come a new curiosity about God's great out-of-doors and a deeper appreciation for the wildlife and beauties of nature in all seasons of the year.

Casting and Fishing

Each year more people go fishing than participate in any other outdoor sport. The U. S. Fish and Wildlife Service quotes a figure of over twenty million, determined by actual survey. Fishing is enjoyed by young and old, rich and poor, in every section of the country. It has the same appeal whether done on a small stream, big river, shallow pond, or deep lake. It has the same value as a leisure-time pursuit for the small boy fishing daily on his father's farm pond or nearby creek as it does for the adult spending a two-week vacation, fishing a wilderness lake in a national forest.

The types and methods of fishing vary according to the personal desires, equipment, and ability of the fisherman. The most elementary form is fishing from a bank or a boat with a line tied to the end of a cane pole. This is commonly referred to as still fishing, the bait usually being live minnows or worms. When the rod and reel is used instead of the cane pole, the fisherman's ability to control the line and bait is greatly increased even though no more or no larger fish may be taken. The rod and reel, rather than the cane pole, has developed into standard fishing tackle for taking game and pan fish in fresh or salt water, whether by still fishing with natural bait or by casting and retrieving artificial lures and flies.

Kinds of Fishing

Fishing tackle and methods may be grouped into four classes: bait, fly, spin, and surf casting.

Bait casting is done with a relatively short, springy rod and revolving spool reel. The weight of the lure causes the line to play off the spool reel which revolves during the cast.

Spin casting is bait casting with a fixed or stationary spool reel, especially adapted for extremely light lures.

Fly casting is done with a stiff, thin rod, seven to ten feet long, and a heavy line that pulls the leader and fly through the air during the cast. The reel is merely a line holder and is not operated except between casts when the line is stripped or rewound.

Surf casting is for ocean-shore fishing, using an extra long, heavy, stiff rod that is cast with both hands. Reels capable of holding lines up to 200 or 300 feet are used and they may be either the revolving or fixed spool type.

Many of the twenty million boys, girls, and adults who fish every year have only moderate success. This is largely because of improper equipment and undeveloped angling techniques. The most important single contributing factor to successful fishing is successful casting. Successful casting means delivering the bait to the area in which the fish may be caught with ease and accuracy and without entangling the line, snapping off hooks, or endangering the safety of the caster or his companions. Less casting is required when still fishing than when using artificial bait. Even so, still fishing requires a certain degree of skill in casting to deliver the bait and line to the water. Fishing with artificial lures is ninety per cent casting and requires proper equipment and technique.

When the essential skills of angling are taught to school-age people, fishing becomes a more satisfactory leisure-time activity. Pupils who have been taught to cast and fish are more likely to enjoy the outdoors because of successful fishing experiences. When given an opportunity to learn the techniques of the sport while in school, more pupils go fishing more often and with greater success. Moreover, learning to cast is fun.

How To Start

Of the two practical ways of conducting casting programs, one—the casting club—is highly desirable in many school situations. Its purpose is to bring together a group of pupils who have a common interest in the outdoors (especially fishing) and to give them an opportunity to learn angling techniques, primarily casting. The casting club is organized and run the same as other school clubs. Meetings may be held before or after school or during an activity period. The club is where the members learn casting skills and fishing techniques, and where they plan other related activities such as field trips to nearby fishing waters. Equipment may be furnished by the individual or by the club.

The second way of sponsoring a casting program is as a curricular activity in a physical education class. This is desirable whether or not there is a casting club in the school. If there is a casting club, its activities fit in nicely. Skills and techniques may be taught in the class, and competition and field trips may become the major activity of the club. Casting may be offered as a full-time physical education activity for a term or semester, or it may be given for a part of a term as one of the several skills taught for use in outdoor activities, such as camping, archery, gun handling, and water safety. Also it is highly desirable for physically handicapped pupils whose outdoor activities are limited.

Equipment

The equipment needed is rods, reels, lines, practice plugs and flies, and casting targets. Targets are either tubular metal rings, thirty inches in diameter, for water, or wooden or metal disks of the same size for lawns and gym floors. The equipment requires little storage space and does not take long to set up or put away. It may be procured in the same way as other physical education and athletic equipment.

Considerable care must be given to the selection of rods and reels so they will function properly when put to their intended use. Tackle sold for fishing is the same as that used for practice casting and for casting competition. Almost all rods are of glass construction. They are durable, need the minimum of maintenance, and are inexpensive. There are so many sizes, shapes, and kinds of reels that a novice fisherman is often confused when making a selection. Reels should be light but durable, made to withstand wear, and simple to operate.

It is extremely important that reels be used for the kind of fishing for which they were intended. For example, many reels are made for still fishing rather than for casting artificial lures. They look like casting reels; but, because of the construction of the frame, spool, and gears, they are not suitable for casting. Those designed for casting have light spools,

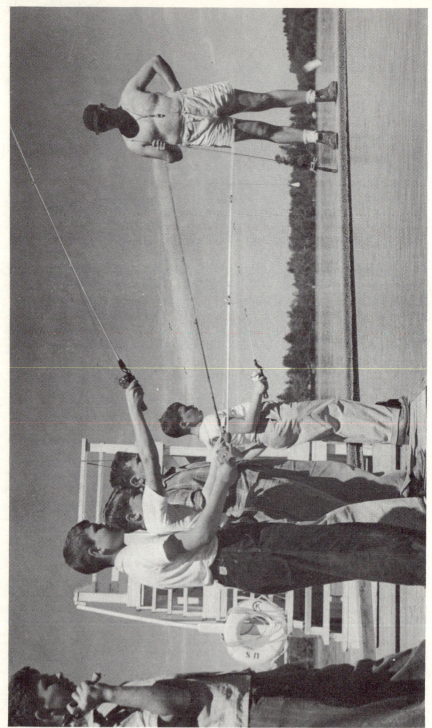

Students learn the skill of bait casting.

large arbors, precision-cut gears, and small handles. They work equally well for still fishing or for casting artificial lures, and are the ones to be used in school casting programs. (Space does not permit a listing of specifications for equipment needed for such programs. This information may be obtained by consulting the Associated Fishing Tackle Manufacturers, fishing tackle salesmen, expert fishermen, fishing tackle manufacturers' catalogues, and manuals such as the one on casting published by the AAHPER for use in the Outdoor Education Project.)

Cost of the Program

There are three phases of a casting and angling program to consider. *First,* casting has value as a skill to be taught. It is easy to learn; pupils with normal coordination acquire the skill readily and improve rapidly with only a few minutes' daily practice. This improvement may continue over a period of months or even years, and may be measured by standards classifying casters according to scores and achievement. Casting is practical to teach because it can be done on a gym floor, on a lawn, or on water. Swimming pools are excellent for water casting.

Second, casting is a highly desirable competitive sport. Pupils may compete with each other on an informal basis. Boys—and girls, too—may stand side by side and test their ability to cast at targets. Or, organized casting tournaments may be conducted according to the rules and regulations set up by the National Association of Angling and Casting Clubs. The NAACC is the control organization for the sport of casting. Through it may be secured rule books, equipment, and appropriate awards for those competing in tournaments. Tournament events test casting for distance and accuracy, with the major emphasis on accuracy.

The word "Skish" has come to be almost synonymous with the term "tournament casting." Originally "Skish" was used to identify tournament events that required standard fishing tackle rather than specialized equipment. In the past few years fishing tackle has been perfected to the point where over-the-counter tackle functions as well as any that is specially made. Now, practically all competition is with standard equipment and the only difference between Skish and other accuracy casting is in scoring. In Skish, a perfect cast has to be made at the target to score points, while in other accuracy casting the caster is given credit for near misses. For example, near misses lose points according to the number of feet the plug or fly lands from the target. In both types of event, the system of scoring is so well defined and easily judged that competitors may score and judge each other.

Carry-over Value

Third, the school-casting program provides an activity with exceptional carry-over value. Students learn the skills of casting while in school, join in the fun of competition with fellow students, and use the skills that are acquired through the activity as a recreational pastime the rest of their lives. Fishing not only serves as a common interest for young companions, outdoor club members, and business associates, but it also is often the main activity of a family group vacationing and camping.

A casting program carries over not only into life after school years, but also into many other outdoor activities such as camping, hiking, scouting, boating, and water safety. To cover the subject adequately some outdoor safety instruction must be included. The program offers an opportunity to teach both water safety and safety practices dealing directly with the use of tackle.

Finally, a casting program leads into related activities such as rod making and repair, fly tying, and camp cooking. Projects such as earthworm raising, the propagation of minnows, and field trips to nearby parks, forests, and streams may be used in conjunction with a casting program as an outdoor approach to science and conservation education.

Archery

The fascination of human beings for shooting bows and arrows is so natural and universal, one almost suspects the coordinations to be basic neural patterns of the species *homo-sapiens*. The lure of archery for those properly initiated is inescapable. Like victims of cupid's darts, archers, once hit by the love of this sport, find archery a life-lasting challenge in their hearts.

Abandoned in warfare since the advent of gunpowder, it is now said to be our fastest growing sport. Instead of giving all the emphasis to such team sports as football, basketball, and baseball, the programs in recreation and physical education of modern high schools and colleges are including archery and other sports that can be continued profitably during our expanding leisure time. To understand why this sport is developing so rapidly in secondary school and college curricula, consider the following statements. Archery:

1. *Is interesting to people of all ages.*
2. *Can be easily adapted to different ages, sizes, and sexes* since bows are made with different drawing weights or pressures, and arrows of different lengths. A small girl gets great satisfaction from shooting her 15-pound bow. An eighty-year old keeps his interest and youth by shooting his 20-pound bow at a target in the back yard. The strength of the strongest football player is challenged by shooting a hunting bow of 45-80 pounds or an elephant bow of one hundred pounds drawing weight.
3. *Is well adapted for use in the individual physical education program,* for the same reasons as those in 2 above. Persons with many different types of physical defects can enjoy archery throughout their lives provided their arms and hands are normal.
4. *Can be enjoyed alone (trying to beat one's own record), or in a group.*
5. *Is an excellent family sport.* Parents and children, each with their own archery tackle, are welcomed at the target archery range of

school or city recreation department, at the field archery course range of the local field archers club, or on a roving expedition of their own hills and through meadows and woods with a picnic at the edge of a brook.

6. *Is an excellent co-educational sport.*

7. *Is an all-season sport:* spring and summer for challenging practice and tournaments in both target and field archery; fall and winter for hunting with the bow. Hunting and roving in deep snow with snowshoes just adds more challenge, adventure, and fun.

8. *As William H. Kilpatrick[4] would say, is a "leading-on activity."*
   a. Its lure, lore, and skill are life-time challenges.
   b. It leads on into conservation study and practice. Its philosophy is one of good sportsmanship relative to hunting game.
   c. It leads on into the area of *crafts* since all archers in a short time learn how to make their own bow-strings, repair arrows, and many of them make their own bows, arrows, and other items of archery tackle. This leads on to the creative designing of new types of bows and arrows. This, of course, happens in home, basement, school, and recreation shops, as well as carrying over into the hobby shops of camps and clubs.
   d. The concomitant learnings are many and varied, stimulating interests in trees and their uses as one learns the different native woods that make bows—osage orange, yew, Tennessee red cedar, hickory, sassafras, *etc.* One learns the characteristics of these woods by seeking them in their native surroundings, cutting them, seasoning them, and fashioning them into bows. One is also sometimes led abroad in the study of foreign bow-woods and arrows.
   e. It frequently leads on to the study of fascinating and complicated problems of physics as one designs new bows with greater cast and flatter trajectory.

9. *Done in proper form, causes a wholesome stretching and relaxing of the cramped, fatigued muscles that keep us humped many hours a day over our desks and work benches.* It necessitates holding heads and chests high, and strengthens the muscles that hold us in good posture.

10. *Places a premium on the individual's willpower, muscular strength, and neuromuscular control; and gives one the keen satisfaction of seeing the arrow fly true as a result of one's own effort—and this leads on to ever higher adventure.*

11. *With well-trained instructors, is one of the safest of sports.* Proper interests, knowledge, attitudes, and skills in archery must be learned by all who would enjoy this challenging sport. Therefore,

---

[4] Kilpatrick, W. H., *Source Book in the Philosophy of Education.*

these must be taught by trained teachers and leaders *so well* that, when people engage in archery, they will shoot the proper way, which is the safe way.

With well-trained instructors, archery is easily and effectively taught even in large physical education sections or classes of thirty to forty pupils. It is easy to grade archery objectively since the arrows are scored by points according to whether they hit the bullseye or in the five colored rings surrounding it.

Rainy-day classes are more than filled with lectures on history of archery, showings of old and new types of bows and arrows and their advantages and disadvantages; of movie films and stripfilms contrasting good form and bad form; conducting a form clinic, testing students on rules, and their ability critically to analyze the shooting form of others.

The Archery Club Approach

Archery can also be taught very effectively in the high school through a co-educational archery club if the leader or faculty sponsor is well trained, an expert performer, and an enthusiastic hobbiest. With the club approach, making one's own tackle in the school shop is a natural development, as well as field trips to city, county, or state park archery ranges. Trips to field archery club ranges and to forests and fields on informal roving and hunting expeditions in season are easily arranged. School archery clubs frequently build their own field archery courses of fourteen or twenty-eight targets on their own school forest land, on a state park or forest, or on the land of an interested farmer or landowner glad to lend the land for such a worth-while purpose. The school archery club should welcome contacts with other clubs in the community, engage in tournaments with them, give joint public demonstrations, and join forces to conduct archery clinics for the instruction of children, youth, and adults in the community and cooperate with the city recreation departments in conducting archery tournaments. Whether archery is taught through physical education classes or recreational clubs, many interesting tournaments can be conducted both for boys and girls in many standard and special events in both target and field archery.

Field Archery Versus Target Archery

In target archery one shoots various rounds which consist of specified numbers of arrows at particular known distances from the targets. In this kind of archery also, either "the point of aim" or a "sight" on the bow is used as a scientific aid for aiming from the different known distances. In field archery, however, no artificial aiming device of any kind is used, and all distances shot are unknown to the archer. This method of shooting, with its anchor position on the face closer to the eye than for target archery, is called "instinctive." It is the way Amerindians and all primitive peoples tended to shoot. For short hunting shots up to forty or fifty yards with distances unknown, instinctive shooting can be very accurate and effective. However, both target and field archery take long, regular, and constant practice for the most satisfying results. Both field archery and target archery should be taught in secondary-school programs. There is a place for both types. In fact, field archery (the least frequently taught) is much the most popular phase of archery today and is responsible for the present tremendous development of public interest in archery.

Equipment

Equipment for a school or club archery program is relatively inexpensive. Satisfactory lemonwood and fiber-glass bows can be purchased for about eight dollars a piece. Arrows will cost $5 to $7 a dozen; and regulation four-foot diameter target butts, around $14. Very satisfactory standards to hold the targets can be made easily by custodians or the pupils themselves in the school shop. Target faces will cost around three dollars a piece, but they can be made for much less in the school shops out of unbleached muslin or heavy oilcloth.

Community Consultants

In every community the country over, there are archery enthusiasts who will be very glad to help school personnel starting archery in physical education classes or in recreational interest clubs. Find out who these people are from your local recreation director or from the Y's, or Scout's headquarters. Better yet, send one or two of your instructors to the national archery training camp, Teela Wooket Camp, Roxbury, Vermont.

Aquatic and Small Craft Activities in Outdoor Education

The importance of aquatic and small craft instruction in outdoor education is indicated by the fact that an estimated 100 million people go swimming and bathing in the United States annually, and twenty-five million take part in recreational boating. Acquiring skills and knowledge in boating, canoeing, or sailing equips the individual to handle his craft wisely, safely, and skillfully. It trains him in methods of rescuing himself in adverse circumstances or specific mishaps. It prepares him to perform efficiently and well in helping or actually rescuing others who are in difficulty or danger. Possession of this type of skill in handling small craft makes the art in itself a thing to be pursued and enjoyed.

Boating Develops Skills and Attitudes

Sailing a boat challenges the sailor to combine knowledge, skill, and coolheadedness in successfully engaging and utilizing a force of nature. Handling a rowboat may invitingly blend skills of the old-time fisherman with those of the Olympic sculler to become stimulating in itself and attractive in its role of being basic to good seamanship in other types of boats. Safe and courteous handling of out-boards and other types of power craft results from study and application of aspects of seamanship that bring to their possessor a pride in gentlemanly conduct afloat and a desire to uphold and advance the laws and traditions of good seamanship. Efficient canoe handling may involve a range of skills from a basic few

Skill in handling canoes reduces accidents.

to a great number. Attractive to many persons because of the intrinsic wilderness character and timelessness of the craft in a supersonic age, the canoe remains essentially the same as it was many thousands of years ago in the earliest of human hands.

As skills and knowledge in all these activities develop, they often encompass one or more of the numerous special forms of aquatic and small craft activity including the following: competitive swimming, ballet swimming, synchronized swimming, diving, skin diving, diving with self-contained underwater breathing apparatus (SCUBA), surfboarding and paddleboarding, sailboat racing, sailboat cruising, rowboat racing, rowing and sculling, racing in sliding-seat racing shells, rowboat cruising, outboard cruising, outboard racing, inboard-power boat cruising and racing, water skiing, canoe racing, canoe cruising, canoe contests and special activities, white water canoeing, and canoe slalom (white water contest).

In addition, small craft handling is involved extensively in fishing, hunting, camping, nature study, and numerous forms of wilderness exploration and field study.

Safety

If preliminary swimming, water safety, life saving, and small craft handling instruction have been given, all of these activities are safer and more enjoyable. Frequently, however, due entirely to absence of such preliminary training, fishermen, hunters, and others lose their lives. In nearly all instances, the most elementary form of knowledge and skill would have prevented the loss of life. Safety instruction, therefore, must be a primary element in this phase of outdoor education.

In planning a program of outdoor education, school officials will find the agencies and organizations with programs and facilities happy to cooperate. In a great number of instances, excellent cooperation on a community level has been going on for many years. In some instances, great advancement in program has come about through similar cooperation on a state-wide level.

A survey of approximately 300 secondary schools and colleges conducted by the Outdoor Education Project of the American Association for Health, Physical Education, and Recreation and the Outboard Boating Club of America in cooperation with Michigan State University indicates that boating instruction is finding its place in the curriculum. It can be done as a club activity or in connection with other class activities, but, in any event, it will meet the needs of an increasing number of students, who have great interest in one of the nation's most popular outdoor activities.

A school principal, aware of the above facts, is confronted with the problem of how to provide efficiently information and training for his students. Large numbers can be given a minimum of instruction through the use of films. The American Red Cross has several films on swimming and water safety and one on boating and canoeing safety. These may be borrowed from local Red Cross chapter offices. The U. S. Coast Guard has available for lending several films dealing with safe operation and legal requirements for pleasure boats, including one film entitled *Outboard Motorboat Safety*. A film, entitled *Small Craft Safety* (black and white, or color, sound, 14 minutes), has been produced by Herbert Kerkow Inc., 480 Lexington Avenue, New York 17, New York. It deals with safe handling, self-rescue, and rescue skills with rowboats, outboards, canoes, and sailboats. The Outboard Boating Club of America, 307 North Michigan Avenue, Chicago 1, Illinois, has produced a filmstrip (sound) entitled *Outboard Handling*.

The best educational results are obtainable through the student participation type of instruction, the complete course being more desirable than teaching lacking organization or done in a cursory manner. Priority should be given to swimming instruction (including water safety). Swimming authorities regard Americans as largely a nation of bathers, with relatively few excellent swimmers. A higher percentage are "good" swimmers, but the majority are able to swim only a little or not at all. This means that most people probably go swimming to relieve their discomfort during hot weather, but not to gain joy and satisfaction from performing the numerous swimming skills, which they do not possess. Through more emphasis on the development of reasonably skillful swimmers, the secondary schools could correct this condition and change the United States from a nation of bathers to one of swimmers.

The Importance of Swimming

It is important to teach swimming also as a basic survival skill indispensable to true safety afloat in small craft. Life jackets and similar devices are important even for skilled swimmers in certain types of situations but they should not be regarded as outright substitutes for swimming ability. Swimming ability ideally should be held as the prerequisite for entry into any type of small craft activity.

In developing a swimming instruction program without existing school operated facilities, the secondary-school principal will usually seek the cooperation of local organizations and agencies having such facilities and program. Often the actual instructional task may be delegated to the various organizations, with the school providing encouragement, promotional support, recognition of work accomplished, and guidance to the over-all community effort.

Many schools have found the American Red Cross swimming and life saving courses ideal for their purposes because they contain the necessary elements and are acceptable and uniform throughout the nation. The swimming courses are graduated: beginner, intermediate, swimmer, and advanced swimmer. There is a junior life saving course for children from twelve to fifteen years, and a senior life saving course for those sixteen years or older or who are in or above the eleventh grade of school.

The Red Cross *Basic and Advanced Survival Swimming Courses* are designed to prepare young people of or near military age to be safe while in or on the water. These courses are excellent for fishermen, hunters, and other outdoor sportsmen. The *Basic Survival Swimming Course* is for nonswimmers and novices. It is particularly designed for boys and girls who have reached secondary school without having learned to swim. It is appealing and far more acceptable to them than is the regular beginners course, which they regard as being for small children.

The above courses are taught by water safety instructors who are trained and qualified in courses conducted in local Red Cross chapters, at selected colleges and universities, and at Red Cross National Aquatic schools. Completion certificates for all these courses are issued by the local chapter or area office.

Piloting Courses

If local interest is in the larger types of small craft, the cooperation of the U. S. Power Squadrons should be sought. They offer free instruction to the public in the form of a *piloting course*. Other courses available to Power Squadron members are: seamanship, advanced piloting, junior navigation, navigation, weather, motor maintenance, and sail. This organization may be contacted locally or at its national headquarters, P. O. Box 510, Englewood, New Jersey.

The United States Coast Guard and Coast Guard Auxiliary provide instruction to the public in seamanship, piloting, motor maintenance, aids to navigation, rules of the nautical road, life saving, and accident prevention. Details are available from the Director of Auxiliary at the nearest Coast Guard District Headquarters, or from United States Coast Guard, Washington 25, D. C.

Without a doubt the outboard motor boat is the most popular type of small craft on the current boating scene. The Outboard Boating Club of America, which is also headquarters for the American Water Skiing Association, has the following educational materials available: *Outboard Handling* (a booklet) ; *What's a Boatload?* (a leaflet); *Use Commonsense Afloat* (a leaflet; also a poster) ; *Outboard Handling* (a filmstrip) ; and *The Water Skier* (a periodical) .

Building on a whole generation of experience in teaching boating and canoeing safety, the American Red Cross during the last few years has developed a well-rounded program of course instruction in handling the smaller types of small craft; namely, canoes, rowboats, small outboards, and small keelless sailboats. The courses are as follows: (1) *Basic Boating Course* (rowboat handling and optional outboard handling content); (2) *Basic Canoeing Course;* (3) *Basic Sailing Course*. There is a detailed instructor's manual for each of these courses. The content of each falls into four major categories: safe handling, self rescue, skills to use in helping or rescuing others who are in trouble, and ways to apply the basic skills interestingly and safely. The courses are taught by *boating instructors, canoeing instructors,* and *sailing instructors,* respectively.

Winter Sports

Winter sports may be divided into two types: snow sports and ice sports. Snow sports include recreational skiing, competitive ski-racing and ski-jumping, snowshoeing, skijoring, recreational sledding, competitive bob-sledding, toboganning, and many different kinds of games, stunts, and contests. Ice sports include skating for fun, skate-racing, skate-sailing, ice-hockey, ice-shinney, figure-skating, curling, and various skating games, stunts, and contests.

In recent years there has been an ever-increasing interest and participation in these winter outdoor activities not only by those who live where there is snow and ice, but also by those living outside the snow and ice belt who, out of curiosity, have ventured a vacation in winter where these sports thrive.

A recent study by the Research Committee of the Central Association for Physical Education of College Women shows that ice skating and skiing are used more commonly after college graduation than they were during college years. These interests have generated a need for programs of effective instruction and planned experiences for high-school students. Many individuals do not have the knowledge, skills, and appreciations necessary to derive the greatest benefit and satisfaction from these vigorous and highly developmental activities, some of which have been described by enthusiasts as not a sport but a way of life.

Our modern way of living is characterized by an apparently ever-increasing time for leisure and a seemingly parallel commercialization of this leisure in such directions that indulgences threaten our future as a vigorous people. The increasing interest in winter sports may in itself be both a conscious and a subconscious effort to prevent deadly outcomes. At any rate it would seem wise for our educational system to explore and exploit the educational potential of these activities that contain really dynamic development and recreational opportunities for richer living. They are challenge and adventure!

Stimulation of the Spirit

Some of these sports such as competitive skiing, skating, and bob-sledding demand and stimulate the fighting spirit, the keen and fighting mind. What more valuable contribution can a school make to the development of an individual than an enduring spiritedness, a high personal morale? What one of us is not reminded by circumstances, now and then, that living successfully demands coolmindedness and courage in the face of fear? Ski-jumping, the world record of which is perhaps the greatest athletic feat, requires all of these and more. Achieving levels of performance in skiing and skating demands self-discipline; and let us not forget that self-discipline is still the basis for great accomplishment in any worthwhile human endeavor.

These sports tend to promote development of the obedient and efficient body under command of the fighting mind. The body's developed skills, vigor, strength, and endurance become the efficient tools for effective and successful action. Let us not forget, too, that these accomplishments encourage a respect for the human organism that comes with the pursuit and achievement of high development. They lead to self-respect and self-reliance and are some of the tools, which, when put into the individual's hands, give him the power to help himself. Certainly this represents no small assistance to effective democratic living.

These outcomes should be objectives of high caliber leadership, which, with modern knowledge of method, can and should see to it that a far higher degree of skill, vigor, and endurance is reached than is commonly achieved. Furthermore, these sports tend to engender a high regard for excellence, which is a basic value in a people whose welfare depends to a large extent upon the superiority of mind, character, and ability of its leaders. The school can reveal to the individual that the delights of skillful sports movement are as necessary to a richer life as any other special ability he seeks to acquire in his youth. It should deepen and enrich the youth's awareness of the possibilities for development and enduring happiness that lie in these winter recreations.

The writer is reminded of a remark made by a young teacher whom he had helped to learn to ski. This young man said, "You know, the winter is over and I have always dreaded the winter season. Yet somehow I feel different this spring. It is hard to believe, but I am already looking forward with eagerness to next winter." Thus a new adventure in movement became a rich and rewarding experience. It is the opportunity for living on a higher level of enjoyment that our people must discover.

The building and care of ski-slopes, ski-jumps, ski-trails, skating and hockey rinks provide many opportunities for valuable work experience especially for those who have not worked much with their hands. In many localities schools can acquire land adjacent, or close, to the school site upon which can be built these snow and ice facilities. With informed and adequate leadership, the building of these facilities by students can represent an experience of considerable value to the individuals concerned and can be a distinct contribution to the community. It is important to note here that the individual not only builds things, but, in the building, makes himself.

Rich in Social Values and Aesthetic Enjoyment

Winter sports are not only individual in nature but are also rich in social values. They are full of opportunity for fun and learning with others under circumstances which promote good feeling and friendship and deepen understanding. They afford an excellent opportunity for the acquirement of good sportsmanship under trying conditions. They can become sparkling and exciting recreational habits in a wholesome setting.

The writer will long remember Canadian children frolicking with their dogs on slopes at St. Jovite. These children had made simple harnesses for the dogs and had trained them to pull the skier to the top of the slope where dogs and children took off downhill in a swirl of snow and vocal excitement. A more effective and satisfying upski, a happier group, this writer has seldom seen.

Finally, ski-touring across snow-covered fields, streams, and forests discloses numerous vistas of beauty and solitude wholly unknown to those who, unlike their ancestors, have not ventured into the hills and back-road terrain at this time of year.

Winter fairylands unfold before the eyes. Aesthetic feelings and appreciations well up within that enrich life. The varying moods of winter as seen from a picture window are as nothing compared with seeing them while snowshoeing or skiing in the out-of-doors. Actual physical contact with our natural resources of forests, streams, and wildlife, and the local geography surrounding our communities in a winter setting, lead to new appreciations long remembered.

To anyone who has experienced them under conditions of capable leadership and good companionship, winter sports are a gift of satisfactions that endure and a rich source of a better life.

Nature Competencies

Millions of Americans achieve satisfaction out of interests in the out-of-doors. These interests may range from sheer aesthetic appreciation to intensely technical scientific inquiry. The satisfaction gained therefrom is based on what Aldo Leopold called "perception." "Perception" involves the response of people to the variety, complexity, and interrelatedness of natural life. It implies a sensitivity on the part of the perceiver to forms, colors, movements, and sounds. It is related to knowledge in its various aspects, including those principles which give the universe its deepest meaning.

Leisure interests among secondary-school students often become highly specialized. What may have been a general interest at the elementary level, may become an interest in astronomy, mosses, fossils, or some other particular field. The student may, however, retain concern for the interrelationships of all living things to each other and to their environment. The secondary-school student may also develop a high sense of responsibility and stewardship, becoming greatly concerned with problems of conservation.

Many of the knowledges, skills, and attitudes of the regular school science program may now become the basis for leisure-time pursuits. They may be engaged in as personal hobbies, as part of special interest clubs, or as incidental parts of the activities of home, club, or vacation.

Specialized competencies in nature are practically unlimited. The following are but a few of those that involve secondary-school youth.

Outdoor Field Experiences

These experiences may include the exploration of woods and fields along with a group or with a naturalist. Such trips usually are concerned with all aspects of the out-of-doors, with emphasis on ecology, human uses, and Indian and pioneer backgrounds. Some trips may concentrate on specialized fields such as geology, water biology, spring wild flowers, birds, fungi, or trees.

Students may make such trips alone. The many excellent nature field books now available make it possible for one to do a great deal of field study and identification alone. Or students may go in small groups, learning from each other and sharing a fruitful experience. However, going out with a leader who knows and loves the out-of-doors is for many the most satisfying type of field experience.

Special Interest Clubs

Clubs with special interests such as biology, astronomy, or conservation are common in schools. Often the science teachers serve as sponsors. Such clubs may conduct varied programs of demonstrations, talks, discussions, field trips, and conservation projects. Entirely voluntary in membership, the clubs have important educational significance in that they increase knowledge and skills and provide opportunities for vocational exploration. The following are some of the nature activities in some of the specialized fields.

Astronomy
Telescope making
Construction and use of starfinders, sun dials, and miniature planetariums
Observation with or without telescopes
Star photography

Biology
Exploration trips to study water life, reptiles, amphibians, insects, birds, trees, flowers, *etc.*
Wildlife studies of specific areas such as watersheds, lakes, streams, *etc.*
Stream improvement projects
Construction and maintenance of terraria and aquaria
Collections of insects, leaves, *etc.*
Research projects on life histories, distribution, *etc.*
Plant succession

Geology
Field explorations to get acquainted with local geological features
Collecting trips to gather rocks, minerals, fossils
Classifying and mounting of minerals for study and display
Gem polishing (lapidary work)
Mapping

Nature-Related Arts and Crafts
Use of native materials such as clay, wood, stone, and fibres in craft programs
Construction of equipment used in nature programs such as terraria, collecting nets, weather stations, display cabinets, *etc.*
Reproduction or interpretation of nature through photography, painting, sketching, plaster of Paris casts, printing
Displaying of nature materials through simple collections, habitat displays, and museum-type displays with interpretive materials

When the nature proficiencies are engaged in as leisure-time pursuits, we may assume that satisfaction comes to the participant more or less

Students use native materials for furniture and equipment.

directly from the experience. Although the content material and outcome may not be essentially different from those of the classroom, the motivation is internal. Interests of lifetime duration may often result from these experiences.

Outdoor-Related Arts and Crafts

Outdoor-related arts and crafts (also called "nature crafts" or "native crafts") are those that utilize primarily the things that can be found in their natural setting in the out-of-doors—scouring rushes *(Equisetum)*, cattail leaves, dead wood, and grapevine bark are only a few examples of these materials. With the aid of glue, string, a pocket knife, or perhaps a tin can, these things can be transformed into objects of practical use or of esthetic value.

The joy of creating is an important, basic experience for everyone. The size of the undertaking is of little importance. What matters most when using native crafts is for the person to realize that the joy of making something can come from other than commercial sources—and the need for this realization is indeed necessary in this materialistic world of ours.

If nature crafts are to be looked upon as a truly outdoor educational experience, the youth participating will be a part of the craft project from beginning to end, collecting materials, preparing them for use, and then finally changing them from their natural state into a utilitarian or esthetic object. These crafts *can* be carried on in the classroom; but, if the teacher collects the materials herself and brings them in, a great deal of value of nature crafts is lost.

Nature crafts automatically find their niche in a school-camping program and can also grow very easily out of a field trip experience. A unit of study on nature crafts is an excellent way of enriching secondary-school arts and crafts courses. Integrating the native crafts experience into other aspects of the educational program is, of course, a highly desirable thing. It can easily be accomplished in a school camp program or in schools having a core curriculum. Crafts need not always be a major project and limited to a scheduled craft period. Wherever possible, they should grow out of other activities. For example, science students, while studying stream-side growth in the spring and the rebirth of life in vegetation that has been dormant through winter, may end up by making willow whistles from the straight, smooth stems of the "pussy willow."

Although the importance of using native crafts in preference to kit-crafts in a school camp experience is recognized by those interested in outdoor education, it is also apparent that many people resort to transporting material and supplies to the outdoor setting and do such things as woodwork with prepared lumber or even kit crafts because they feel inadequately prepared to carry on any type of nature crafts with their groups. How much more secure we feel when teaching things with which we have had some personal experience! One cannot stress strongly enough the need for actual experimentation on the part of the leader before working with his group, rather than just reading about the proposed project in a nature craft book.

Many leaders working with teenagers have expressed their need for finding nature craft ideas that will appeal to older children. The following are a few craft ideas which have been selected as suggestions for a teenage arts and crafts program. It should be stressed again, however, how important it is for the leader to try these crafts first.

Twig Vases. Glue narrow twigs a bit longer than the height of the can to the sides of a small tuna fish can or other suitable planter. Use a rubber band to help hold the newly glued twigs in place until they are dry. The twigs give a very pretty "picket fence" appearance to the vase or planter.

Black Walnut or Butternut Seed Sections. Using a hack saw, cut slices crosswise through the nut. Hold the saw between your knees or in a vise with the cutting edge up and run the nut back and forth over the saw to cut it. This is unconventional, but it prevents binding which occurs when the nut is held in the vise. If the hacksaw will hold two blades, separate the blades at either end with matchsticks; then two cuts can be made at the same time, insuring even slices. When sanded and waxed these sections make beautiful buttons, earrings, or belts.

Seed Jewelry. Seeds of various sorts—canteloupe, watermelon, corn, *etc.*—can be strung into beautiful necklaces and bracelets. Soak the seeds for an hour or so to allow the needle to penetrate without splitting the seeds. Seeds may also be glued to earring backs to form rosettes.

Fungus Etching. Growing on the sides of trees, stumps, and logs in many parts of the country may be found a woody, shelf-like fungus with a very white underside. Gather these bracket fungi during their growing period, which is approximately April to September. During this time the slightest touch on the underside of the fungus will leave a dark brown mark on a white background. Sketch a picture on this white surface with a twig, knife, or nail within twenty-four hours after picking. Put it aside to dry for about a week. These etched bracket fungi make beautiful decorative pieces.

Log Book Ends. Saw a log about five inches in diameter into eight-inch lengths. Then saw it lengthwise into two half-logs. Scrub the bark. Attach the bark to the wood securely with brads around the edges. Stand each half-log on end and attach a flat, rectangular piece of tin to the underside to be used as a base and to insert under books. Attach felt to the tin to keep it from scratching the table. Designs may be woodburned on smooth, light bark such as birch and beech. The bark may be shellacked if desired.

The alert teacher will see possibilities in many other native media— mats woven of cattail leaves, ceramics from native clay, wall hangings and planters created from driftwood, dyes made from berry juices, and lapel pins from seeds, whittled wood, types of fungi, or feathers. The opportunities are limited only by one's imagination.

Orienteering

A remarkable and effective new program for creating and maintaining a lasting interest in self-education for outdoor life is gaining wide popularity in the schools of several countries. It may sound strange but in the term "orienteering" itself is found one of the answers to the question why this program has had such success. Instead of talking to youngsters about map-and-compass instruction you talk about orienteering. And immediately it sounds like a sport, a game—something that is fun, enjoyable, instead of some kind of regimented teaching.

Popular in Europe

This program of map-and-compass study was first introduced in Sweden in 1917-18. It quickly spread through Europe as both an educational and sports program. Now orienteering is a compulsory part of the curriculum in Sweden and Norway. It has developed into one of the most popular national competitive sports for men, women, and children from nine to ten years of age and over, not only in Sweden and Norway but also in Denmark, Finland, and Switzerland. Five years ago its educational values were recognized in Canada, and orienteering became an adjunct to courses in social studies and geography in the schools of the Province of Ontario. In the United States the program of orienteering is now in general use by the Boy Scouts, the Girl Scouts, Camp Fire Girls, other youth organizations, and also by camp counselors. It is involving an ever increasing interest and acceptance among some secondary schools.

Skill Learning and Sport

Orienteering can be included in an appropriate place in the school's outdoor program. It can be divided into two main parts: first, there are educational, theoretical, and instructional aspects that develop skill in map reading and love for the out-of-doors. And this is where the schools should come in more actively. *Second,* there is the expanded development of this instruction into a competitive sport. There are different variations, ranging from simple recreative games and contests, preferably combined with conservation and nature lore, to the more intricate cross-country races, where map and compass is used to locate certain control stations in unknown territory.

To summarize, orienteering has made the teaching of map and compass easier and more effective; it has made the learning more enjoyable and interesting. On the basis of using map and compass, a completely new sport has developed.

Map Reading

In the orienteering program, the theoretical side is de-emphasized, especially at the introductory level. Children want to know the objectives before they enjoy learning the finer points and parts. Map reading should, therefore, never be just that! In orienteering, map reading is just a part of the whole process with much practical use in games and fun exercises, organized in such a way that there is a permanent contact in the pupils' minds between the theoretical teaching and the purpose of it. Orienteering, with its many practising games, gives the fundamental teaching in map-and-compass use a meaning from the beginning; the learning becomes a part of the fun and is acquired more rapidly. The knowledge itself becomes more solid.

An Outdoor Avenue

When youngsters have learned how to use map and compass intelligently, it does not necessarily mean that they will ever get interested in orienteering as a competitive sport. But they have gained confidence in their own ability and skill, and they have developed proficiency and experience in fending for themselves in the woods. By doing so, they have unconsciously assimilated a favorable attitude towards outdoor life of all kinds, which will give them lots of enjoyment and help to create and maintain their physical fitness from childhood throughout their lives. And there you have the greatest value of orienteering.

Principals of secondary schools who desire to consider the merits of orienteering as a possible new subject to include in the curriculum will find informative and organized training materials at their command. These were developed with the cooperation of educators and leaders in youth organizations.

The outdoors becomes the classroom for skiing instruction.

CHAPTER III

Facilities and Resources for Outdoor Education

"In the woods we return to reason and faith."—Ralph Waldo Emerson

1. LANDS, PARKS, AND AGENCIES

THE application of the meaning of the word *facilities,* as stated in the dictionary, applies best to outdoor education programs. Therein it states that facilities are generally physical things which promote the ease of any action, ease of operation, or course of conduct. Facilities for outdoor education, such as lands, certainly do promote ease in the course of conducting such programs. Almost all public lands, their curtilage, and other accommodations lend themselves to these purposes, as often do some privately owned lands.

Available Lands and Parks

For the most part, public lands are dedicated for specific uses in accordance with statutes which were adopted before the current surge to the out-of-doors took place. However, the purposes for which they were dedicated are stated in broad terms, and, therefore, by implication they include the purposes of and services for outdoor education. Many of these public lands, especially parks, were dedicated for the public enjoyment of natural beauty and for the perpetual preservation of their natural characteristics for enjoyment by the public. Some were, and today others are, dedicated to preserve their historical association and significance, and as places for the enjoyment of public recreation. These concepts might easily include the purposes of education, and beyond that, the *enjoyment of education!* Cognition is given to the real and thrilling enjoyment found in outdoor education.

Some of the public lands which have been used for outdoor education include parks, forests, refuges, reservations. The experimental woodlots, nurseries, and similar areas on state-supported college campuses; similar lands owned by school districts; and many others of this kind provide outdoor laboratory opportunities.

In addition to these, there are properties in private ownership. They vary in size even more than the public lands, from small individual farms and clubs to the immense acreages of lumber, mining, ranches, and other commercial enterprises. Some of them are already under use. Others hold promise for use in the near future. It is a fact, for example, that the

91

Weyerhaeuser Timber Company of Tacoma, Washington, has opened the doors to its vast holdings to the public for outdoor activities. Although the activities are currently labeled as recreational, those who are aware of the educational potential perceive the obvious parallel for educational experiences in camping, hunting, fishing, hiking, skiing, bird watching, archery, exploring, sightseeing, picking berries, collecting rocks, photography, and many other activities of this kind.

The Company, in making its lands available, seeks and hopes to educate people properly in the use of the out-of-doors. Could there be a better way to accomplish this than by outdoor education programs in collaboration with professional educators? What a perfect opportunity of mutual concern and interest, citizenship!

Perhaps it would be of interest to read the reprint of an address presented by Frederick Billings, Public Recreation Administrator of Weyerhaeuser, to the thirty-sixth annual meeting of the National Conference on State Parks[1]. He states that " . . . people are going to use our lands for outdoor activities . . ." Then he touches upon a number of principles that apply to education's ideal of better citizenship, less vandalism, and more enjoyment of living for the people of today and tomorrow.

The nature and interpretive programs of the National Park Service are well known. These programs, which have been popular for many years, are increasing. State parks and other park administrations are adding them to their over-all park programs. The interpretive program, for example, has been extended to include four major parks administered by the Province of Ontario, Canada. It is a trend all over the nation, and outdoor education has the possibility of reaping much benefit from it.

Expansion of Park Services

It is encouraging for outdoor education to note that, in the face of increasing, heavy park use and strained budget emphasis on repairs and maintenance, some park authorities are adding interpretive and public relation services because of their *educational value*. Naturalists are being added to park staffs to conduct park patrons on guided tours and trips. In addition there are building programs including the construction of museums, zoological gardens, group camps, and other facilities. Park administrators are also preparing exhibit and display materials, and have increased the attractiveness and availability of descriptive folders and brochures. Some are conducting, or may be encouraged to conduct, regular radio and television programs on land use and local history and wildlife; talks on travel and exploration to local points of interest; tales of fishing, hunting, and adventure. All of this activity is of value as facilities and resources for outdoor education.

---

[1] *Planning and Civic Comment*, December 1956, pp 51-60, American Planning and Civic Association and National Conference on State Parks, 901 Union Trust Building, Washington 5, D.C.

Many of these park services are recent developments and indicate changes in administrative policy. A policy change is noted in the Tennessee State Park system. State park naturalists were used to assist camping agencies using state park group-camp facilities in teaching appreciation of their camp environment. This service is now available through the Tennessee Game and Fish Commission, which provides group-camping agencies with a game and fish counselor. Outdoor education programs as *educational projects* under *educational administration* have an obvious opportunity here. A favorable setting for team action with the parks for mutual purposes.

It should be recognized that the facilities on public lands available for public use must be made more desirable. As more park authorities recognize this fact, they will be rewarded with less ruthless wear and destruction by a public that has learned appreciation through more satisfying experiences. Programs of outdoor education could perhaps spearhead this drive for public education. It would be well for park men to cater to the development of outdoor education programs with this end in view. This has been proved, at least in Michigan.

Expansion of Michigan Camps

The Michigan Department of Conservation's Parks and Recreation Division at first provided little more than bare essentials in group camps administered as state park facilities. Now it has refurnished and insulated the old camps and constructed new ones to encourage use the year around. Dishes and utensils are furnished. There is electric power and fuel oil heat. It was found that better facilities, in terms of quality, invite more use, which in the long run returns dividends by way of proper use of lands and facilities. Better understanding and sympathy is promoted for conservation policies and problems. Excerpts from the magazine, *Michigan Conservation,* January-February 1957, in an article titled "Classrooms in the Snow at State Parks," by Harold Guillaume illustrate this point.

". . . growing, interesting and instructive educational program now under way in a number of Michigan's state parks . . . takes an annual 8,000-9,000 youngsters . . . and gives them a week or more in a natural setting . . . These youngsters hardly notice during their week away from (school) classes that schooling, that insidious process, is still going on . . .

"The camps work in a very simple and inexpensive manner. Any community school system can contract with the conservation department to send its junior graders to any of the state's various group camps . . . in conveniently-sized groups, the youngsters are taken by car or school bus and deposited at the camp . . .

"During this week, the youngsters are supervised by teachers from their own school system and by resource personnel from the department and other agencies . . .

"They go on hikes and learn woods lore . . . plant trees and stage cook-outs . . . go fishing and hold pint-sized nature expeditions . . . learn the best way to build a camp fire, how to cut wood and make protective lean-tos, how to catch fish through the ice . . . learn what is meant by a healthy, productive forest and how it needs care and harvest . . . They visit local installations such as sawmills, forest fire control stations, tree farms, game cover plantings, and whatever other activities the area offers . . .

"This unique program started in Michigan in 1948, when leaders from the Department of Public Instruction and the Conservation Department found that the . . . group camp program could be put to work in the winter for school camping. Group camps were originally designed to accommodate summer groups . . . the so-called fall-winter-spring 'off season' now sees camps visited by twice as many . . . as use these facilities in the summer . . .

"They (educational leaders) see in school camping a method of getting students involved—with both feet—in studies of social science . . . biology . . . physical education . . . and other 'academic' pursuits . . .

"Youngsters also complete many projects for the cause of conservation during their winter camping. They build dams for small floodings and plant eroded hillsides . . . build brushpiles for rabbits . . . also for fish . . . placed on lake ice to sink during the spring thaw and provide underwater habitat for game fish . . .

"The conservation department, too, would like to continue and expand this cooperative educational program that makes such a splendid use of a natural resource. Department leaders see school camping as a way to touch our growing citizenry . . . with the principles of conservation and outdoor living . . . But one thing is certain . . . the present program will continue to hold a secure place in the plans of many educators . . ."

The activities mentioned in the foregoing excerpts suggest the kinds of outdoor education use group-camp facilities afford and the kinds of resources available. Attention was purposely directed to them in the selected quotations, as well as to the cooperative arrangement enjoyed by the two state governmental departments of public instruction and conservation. It is an example of excellent rapport from which outdoor education has prospered.

Another classification of camp facilities includes those owned by agencies and private operators. These are Boy Scout, Girl Scout, Campfire Girls, 4-H club, YMCA, YWCA, church-owned, and other camps. Although many of them are not constructed for cold weather seasons, they are satisfactory for use in early fall and late spring.

It is encouraging to know that some agencies involved in new camp construction projects are building all-weather facilities so that their own programs may be extended. Since the agencies conventionally conduct their camp activities on weekends, they would probably be glad to make arrangements for use of their camps on school days when there would be no conflicts for use. The locations of these camps, generally on a lake and in a woods, provide ideal outdoor settings.

Learning Potentials on the Land

There are still other facilities, both publicly and privately owned, that may be utilized for outdoor education programs. Some facilities may serve only specific purposes, perhaps, and by their very nature are limited to certain kinds of use. Their potential should not be overlooked. For example, consider old cemeteries. They are an important historical link between bygone pioneering days and today's modern world. Old cemeteries have proved to be interesting in many ways through the reflections of students and teachers while reading and musing about the inscriptions and dates on the headstones and tablets. At the risk of again diverting emphasis from facilities to activities, a few outdoor activities that may take place at old cemeteries are mentioned.

Social histories and family associations are revealed, as well as facts and fears, beliefs, and shattered hopes. Follow-up study is self-encouraged as interest mounts concerning high infant mortality as well as high mortality among young adults as indicated on headstone dates. These facts penetrate and motivate the minds of school children. The stones marking the graves of veterans of wars often stimulate further study. The craftsmanship of stone cutting, former and new methods; the uses of granites, marble, soapstone, sandstone, and other rock materials; all of these may awaken new interest and more genuine desire for learning.

Then there are gravel pits and stone quarries from which a history older than man may be unfolded and related to today's world. The uses of the products of gravel pits and quarries, or the fact that their products may no longer be of important use, tell stories of their own and promote good learning situations. The search for fossils at these sites, as well as in the surface rock and drift waste piles around mines, is fascinating and is fun. Yet, learning continues.

The shores of large lakes and the seaside have many potentials. They, like the other areas mentioned, whether in public or private ownership, if their use is permitted, afford an unlimited fascination for "pebble pups" and others interested in collecting and examining specimens of stones, rocks, shells, semi-precious stones and gems, ores, driftwood, and other objects which await their discovery. These are opportunities for educational enjoyment. Some youngsters, having had this opportunity as youths, may become professional lapidaries, geologists, mining engineers, or scientists—or better teachers. Above all, however, whether these outdoor learning experiences will mold their future professions or not, there is something intangibly valuable about them throughout a lifetime which is based upon the human associations in these experiences, and that may help to mold a desirable character.

It is really surprising to realize that there is such an abundant supply of facilities and resources on hand for outdoor education programs. The resources go far beyond the facilities *per se*. Indeed, resources are a strengthening factor for initiating outdoor education programs. This is true particularly of resource personnel. Personnel is available at all levels and comprises a heterogeneous group in terms of professions, avocations, interests, abilities, and areas of specialization. Still, their various talents often blend and harmonize for their use in outdoor education projects. Resource personnel may be utilized as individuals or as a team. Experience has demonstrated this fact conclusively.

Resource Personnel

Resource personnel sometimes is mustered advantageously on a team basis, the mechanics of which become easier with experience. There are all sorts of combinations of resource personnel teams, obtained sometimes by special committees assigned to this responsibility in the organization of an outdoor education venture. At other times a program director may assume this responsibility, and in cooperation with group leaders (classroom teachers), coordinates services and contributions of the resource personnel obtained for the program. An Associated Press newspaper account is a helpful illustration.[2]

Mr. Henderson describes the program of Michigan's Iron River Junior High School, which merited the Nash Conservation Award for teacher Hoyt L. Ferm. In sequences the students learn about animals from mounted specimens, then proceed to related studies of environment; trees, streams and watersheds, and their management. He states that "The Michigan Department of Conservation pitches in with movies and with field men. So do many individuals and organizations in Ferm's community, now conditioned and at least partly populated by his graduates. Trappers tell about trapping . . . stone collections lead to geology, and that brings a trip to the area's mines, and practical explanations by mining engineers and geologists. Police officers officiate during a course of safe gun handling, the local fire chief lends authority to forest fire fighting . . ."

As indicated above, often the resource personnel representing public agencies and private concerns may form or be formed into teams to make their services more effective. It is common for governmental technicians in fisheries, parks, forests, and soils to work together, just as it is for representatives of tackle and boat manufacturers and hunting arms to work jointly to provide services and demonstrations. These field representatives of government and of private manufacturers stand ready and are on call to serve outdoor education situations. There is much learning to be had about our natural resources and about firearms, fishing tackle, boats, outboard motors, tents, camping equipment, winter sports equipment, outdoor clothing and sportswear and gear.

---

[2] *"Pupils Learn About Field and Forest"* by Dion Henderson, Associated Press Staff Writer, *The State Journal*, Lansing, Michigan, Sunday, January 27, 1957.

When the local level does not seem to have resource personnel available, or when the local level cannot provide desired resource personnel, it becomes the responsibility of a higher level—often the state—to give assistance to outdoor education programs. This responsibility may be vested in the state department of public instruction (chief state school officer), the extension services departments of state universities and colleges, the state department of conservation, bureau of resources, game fish, forests, or the like, state department of health, and others, or combinations of these authorities.

Inter-Agency Councils

Where there are state inter-agency councils for recreation, such as in Michigan, Ohio, Virginia, and others, for example, the availability and the coordination of these services is made quite simple. Inter-agency councils or inter-agency committees are especially effective in organizing procedure to obtain resource personnel and facilities for outdoor education programs. Through the inter-agency operation plan, all the personnel of the inter-agency members become available for services to implement and assist education and recreation projects. The Michigan Inter-Agency Council for Recreation has made significant contributions to outdoor education workshops and institutes at the state level, as well as at the local level, by serving scores of community school camping programs.

The philosophy that the state, under its sovereign authority, has the responsibility and should provide for services that are beyond the province of local government, is generally accepted.

The resources and facilities available for outdoor education programs are practically unlimited. They need but be discovered—and utilized. They are among the unique features found in the variety of outdoor education program patterns. A vitalizing effect results from their use and especially from the use of resource personnel.

There are a variety of resources to complement the facilities. They include the files of informative material, such as descriptive pamphlets and bulletins. They also include the technical data and records compiled over a long period of time, representing many years of professional work and research in natural science subject areas. This material leaps into action by interpretive processes which may be provided by resource personnel.

The personnel representing the many governmental departments engaged in administering publicly owned lands and natural resources, and the personnel from institutions of higher learning are invaluable as resource personnel for outdoor education endeavors. As previously mentioned, there are soil men and geologists and wildlife technicians, and others, at all levels of government and in colleges. They, as instructors and as interpreters, sharing the knowledge and wisdom of their life's work through their documents and informative material, bring life to outdoor education in outdoor learning situations. When invited they usually consent to serve, and enjoy their participation.

The field and office personnel of these departments and institutions use a variety of "tools of the trade," which are also valuable and interesting resources. Some of these tools are quite simple, and others are complicated instruments and mechanical devices. All of them, however, capture learning interests. A surface understanding of their purposes as tools is usually sufficient for the outdoor education student, and students usually comprehend their purposes. The tools range from such simple things as compasses, blazing axes, soil testing kits, surveyors chain, and weather station equipment to Biltmore sticks for scaling timber, Jacob's staff compasses, microscopes, Geiger counters, and others.

Most of the resources available in outdoor education programs are not costly. Materials and tools generally are free or on a loan basis, and, therefore, do not constitute an item of expense. There is no program expense for personnel used for resources, at least not often, for their services to outdoor education is considered to be a normal function of job responsibility.

Teamwork in Outdoor Education

Outdoor education can be made available to all children and youth only if the agencies concerned with education and those having the responsibility for the custody and management of natural resources are the "team" and mobilize their efforts. State and national governmental agencies of education and conservation should lead the way by joint action in making leadership and facilities available in helping schools and colleges, together with professional and voluntary youth serving agencies. The same cooperative pattern is even more important at the community level. In many outdoor programs, the harmony and cooperation is so complete that the identification of educators, conservationists, recreationists, and youth leaders is lost when operating on local action programs. In several instances, state-wide efforts have been spearheaded by joint projects in outdoor education. Such has been the case in Michigan, Ohio, California, New Hampshire, and others. Among the many Federal, state, and local organizations and agencies actively involved in outdoor education efforts of the various states are:

National:
    American Association for Health, Physical Education, and Recreation
    Audubon Society
    American Camping Association
    Isaac Walton League
    National Conference on State Parks
    American Institute of Park Executives
    National Congress of Parents and Teachers
    American Forestry Association
    National Recreation Association
    Boy Scouts of America
    Girl Scouts of America
    American Recreation Society
    National Education Association (Many of the departments)
    National Association of Angling and Casting Clubs

National Association of Secondary-School Principals
The National Rifle Association
The Sporting Arms and Ammunitions Manufacturers' Institute
The Associated Fishing Tackle Manufacturers
The Outboard Boating Club of America
American Red Cross

Federal:

National Parks Service
National Forest Service
U.S. Geographical Survey
National Wildlife Federation
U.S. Army Corps of Engineers
President's Council for Fitness of American Youth
Office of Education

State:

State Office or Department of Public Instruction
State Library
Department of Conservation, Department of Natural Resources
State Forest Commission or Department
State Game and Fish Department or Commission
State Highway Department
State Park Department or Commission
State Beach Commission
State Inter-Agency Council for Recreation
State Land Use Committee
State Health Department
State Police or Highway Patrol
State Department of Economic Development
State University and State College Extension Departments
State Historical Commission
Inter-State Waterways Commission
Conservation—Education Association
Board of Commerce and Trade
Soil Conservation Service
State Camping Association

Local:

County Sanitarian
Sportsman's Clubs
Garden Clubs
Citizens' Development Committee
Metropolitan or County Park Authorities
Civic and Service Clubs
Affiliates of State Recreation Associations
Sheriff and Police Departments

Local Agencies:

4-H Clubs
PTA Clubs
YMCA and YWCA
American Red Cross
The Grange
Historical Societies

The modern school, showing separate wings and structures for year-round community use.

2. School-Community Facilities and Resources

THE facilities and resources for outdoor education must be of many types because of the broad scope of the program. They are to be found in the school plants, in the vicinity of the school, parks and forests, public camp sites, and the resident camp, whether owned or leased by the school district.

The facilities for outdoor education should include certain features and resources such as soil, water, plant, and animal life that provide for opportunities, experiences, and projects on using and conserving natural resources. It is by on-the-land experiences that youth are given a real understanding and appreciation of the teeming life in soil and water as well as how the very existence of the nation is dependent on the water table, the streams, the lakes, and the productivity of the soil. Such experiences with wildlife lay the foundations for understanding and appreciating the essential place of such plants and animals in our living environment and the wise use and conservation of them.

The facilities should include the resources—some indoor as well as outside which can be used for projects and activities in developing and protecting the Nation's most valuable resource—its youth. Such indoor facilities as the crafts shop and the science laboratory may be starting points for outdoor education projects whether it is tying flies or making bows which would lead on into fishing and hunting. Starting a science laboratory may be the beginning of using the outdoors as a living laboratory and a broader understanding of the environment in which we live. Likewise, use can be made of the facilities for physical education, homemaking, health education, and social studies areas which will lead on into outdoor experiences in hiking, scouting, swimming, water safety, providing for food, clothing, shelter, and gaining understanding and appreciation by the living descendents of the pioneers who built the foundations of America. It follows inevitably that from such indoor experiences youth need and should have the great out-of-doors to carry on and acquire the appreciations, knowledges, and skills for outdoor living. On-the-land experiences in the forests, the parks, conservation centers, and camps adds stimulation to many areas of education and brings the goals more closely in line with the stream of life of the community as well as the forces which have built a great democracy.

The Community or Park School

The modern school plant contains many resources and facilities for many outdoor education activities. The park-school concept which envisions the modern building in a park-like setting combines the best features of the school, the park, and the playground. Many such schools have been built in states over the nation since the National Conference on Facilities for Health, Physical Education, and Recreation projected this idea in the publication of its first Guide in 1947. Such plants contain many features and resources that can be used for outdoor education. In such a plant the course of education can follow along with the stream of life in the community. Likewise, the community-school concept makes possible a community-wide curriculum that goes beyond the walls of the building and the boundaries of the site to deal with the problems, the hopes, and the aspirations of a democratic society for the education and development of young citizens.

In both of these concepts, the elementary school is planned and used as a neighborhood center. The site as recommended by the National Facilities Conference would contain at least fifteen acres, which includes such features as a level area for group activities, outdoor cooking, picnics, park and wooded area, and a "polliwog" pond. In many cases the site is larger than the minimum of fifteen acres. Quite often a larger site will cost less than a smaller site. In fact, there is little correlation between the size and the cost of the site in most cases. Furthermore, the cost of purchase and development of the site is usually less than five per cent of the total cost of the building.

Likewise, the junior and senior high schools are planned for use as community centers. The modern secondary-school building contains many facilities that would function in the development and extension of outdoor education projects. The park-like site would contain many features for outdoor education trips and projects. The National Facilities Conference recommends a minimum of twenty-five acres for a junior high school and a minimum of forty acres for the senior high school. The area would include level space for fields and courts and park and wooded areas with trees and water, and other facilities for outdoor cooking, picnics, archery, scouting, and the like.

As with the elementary school, the general practice is to provide sites that are much larger than the minimum. Some schools buy 150 to 250 acres which comprise a whole tract or farm so that the secondary school would be a real community center according to the park-school concept that would provide a large number of newly developed suburban areas the only opportunity for a park. Some schools, of course, provide a school garden within such a tract that gives opportunities for experience with soil, water, plant, and animal projects.

The decentralization of manufacturing, business, and marketing and the persistent movement to the suburban areas has made the construction of modern school plants a national as well as state and local problem. Such construction is going ahead at a rapid rate. One thing is certain. Schools must be built to house the increased population. It is evident that such schools are being built to serve the community and the neighborhoods where the people live. It is, therefore, urgent that imagination, vision, courage, and initiative should be used in planning the community or park school types of plant in a park-like setting which would make possible the conduct of an outdoor education program that vitalizes the whole educational curriculum and forms a cultural bond between the pioneer and his living descendents.

The Resident Camp

The Educational Policies Commission, in its report, *Education for All American Children*,[3] describes the resident camps as a unit of the school system that is planned, built, and operated on the same sound basis as a school in the system. The State Departments of Education and Conservation in Michigan have developed plans for a desirable and functional school camp. The conservation department built such a camp on some of the state lands for use by schools to demonstrate and study the type of a school camp that would function best for such projects. Tyler, Texas, with the cooperation of groups in the community, has built and is operating such a camp on lands owned by the community and adjacent to a water conservation center.

The 1956 publication of the National Facilities Conference *Planning Facilities for Health, Physical Education, and Recreation*[4] contains a whole chapter on the resident camp. It outlines guides for the development of camps for schools and other organizations. It holds to the principle that the program must determine structure and gives information on selecting the camp site, planning the layout and development, and constructing the buildings and facilities.

The selection of the site should be considered in terms of water supply and availability of electricity. The site should be sufficiently large to include areas such as a stream or lake shore, a wooded lot, and geographical and other features essential to camp experiences, such as trails, campfire circles, amphitheatres. The site should have a rolling topography rather than a very rugged or unusually flat surface. The soil should be sandy loam and porous rather than heavy clay. The site should be sufficiently large in size so that outlying camps or more than one camp unit can be located therein.

The functional design of the building would include a space for administration, areas for storage, cooking and serving food, staff quarters, offices, service facilities, and housing units depending upon the population to be served and the program to be conducted.

The resident camp provides individual and group experiences on a 24-hour a day living basis. It provides experiences for youth on a sound educational basis that ties in more closely with home and community life than other areas of education. It is, therefore, a facility that can offer many project and learning experiences that begin in the school and continue on into the life of the community. There are many resources in resident camps that can be leased until such time as the school may decide to build its own camp. Many of the private and organizational types of camps operate only in the summer months. If an arrangement could be made for leasing such camps, the owners could afford to improve

---

[3] *Education for All American Children.* Washington, D. C.: National Education Association, 1948.

[4] *Planning Facilities for Health, Physical Education, and Recreation.* Chicago: The Athletic Institute, 1956. Obtainable from the American Association for Health, Physical Education, and Recreation.

and winterize them so that they would be useful for a large part of the school year. They could be used in many cases during the good winter months or the spring and fall.

Conservation Resources

The forests, state lands, and large parks contain many resources for outdoor education. Some state conservation departments that have had successful experience with such camp sites are exploring the possibilities of developing the sites for use by the advanced camping group from the schools. Such sites could be developed in connection with conservation projects that would provide facilities for youth to gain the knowledge, skills, and appreciations for the conservation of natural resources and for experiences that would be wholesome, healthful, and satisfying. The goals of conservation and those of education could be attained.

Such outlying regions, camps, and state lands are much more accessible than in the past because of better roads and vehicles. America has put education on wheels and used the school bus efficiently, economically, and successfully in taking children where education can be more fruitful for self and society.

The facilities and resources for outdoor education are large, varied and abundant; imagination, courage, and initiative can bring such resources into the lives of all the youth.

3. NATIONAL PROJECTS AND PROGRAMS FOR OUTDOOR EDUCATION

ONE of the encouraging developments in outdoor education is the number of special projects and programs that have been sponsored by a variety of national organizations. Following other newer trends in education, these projects, which are designed for experimentation and action research, not only test the goodness and effectiveness of new programs, but also are instrumental in the more rapid growth of timely educational efforts. The following are illustrative of a number of new developments in outdoor education sponsored by national organizations that have a concern and responsibility for the various types of outdoor programs.

The Outdoor Education Project of the American Association for Health, Physical Education, and Recreation

While outdoor activities have been recognized in good health, physical education, and recreation programs for many years, they have not found their rightful place in the school and college curriculum in the country as a whole. Prompted by the need for leadership in teaching skills, attitudes, and appreciations for a better use and understanding of the outdoors for modern living, the American Association for Health, Physical Education, and Recreation initiated the Outdoor Education Project. Following the effective pattern in cooperative programs by business-industry-education, some of the industries that manufacture outing equipment joined with the Association in the Project by making available grants of funds to carry forward the program. The Associated Fishing Tackle Manufacturers and the Sporting Arms and Ammunition Manufacturers' Institute (SAAMI) have been involved from the beginning in this venture. In 1956-57, the Outboard Boating Club of America made a grant of funds to the Project for a survey of boating instruction in a selected list of schools and colleges in the United States.

Like other important educational programs, a great need is for dynamic leadership in schools and colleges in order that the 37 million boys and girls in schools and the three million youth in schools and colleges may acquire the necessary skills, attitudes, and appreciations for the intelligent use of our resources and for the constructive use of leisure time. It is evident that people cannot fully enjoy and appreciate outdoor activities such as camping, casting, fishing, shooting, hunting, boating, winter sports and others unless they have adequate training. These activities in outdoor living are related, with conservation and safety being integral parts. The Project program, therefore, is designed to intensify and speed up outdoor education programs in schools and colleges through the in-service training for leaders, interpretation of the need for and nature of outdoor education activities, program development, and the preparation of instructional materials.

The American Association for Health, Physical Education, and Recreation, through its staff and other resources, in cooperation with the departments of the National Education Association, the National Rifle Association, state departments of education, conservation agencies, representatives of the cooperating industries, and schools and colleges, is carrying forward the Project program. A national advisory committee, widely representative of school and college administrators and groups interested in outdoor education, helps guide the Project program. The Project, which will operate over a period of years, encompasses the following activities:

1. *Leadership Training.* Regional and state workshops and clinics are conducted for school and college staff members who are interested in developing programs in their own states. Working with the Project staff, the appropriate state agencies, such as the departments of education and conservation, colleges and universities, and professional educational organizations, as well as interested individuals, are in the planning and execution of the workshops. These training ventures combine interpretation; information about how to conduct programs of casting, shooting, camping, boating, and other activities; clinics and instructional methods; use of equipment; and the preparation of material.

2. *Interpretation and Information.* The need for the development of outdoor education programs and the Project's plan of operation are interpreted to school administrators, teachers, and other interested groups through programs, exhibits, demonstrations at conventions,

and articles in educational journals. Many of these are done through the departmental structure of the National Education Association.

3. *Instructional Materials.* Needs for additional instructional materials are being determined and committees are at work preparing instructional guides and audio-visual aids.

The Outdoor Education Project, with its broad emphasis on a variety of activities, is stimulating much interest in the schools and colleges of the nation. It is believed that this is a sound venture because it stresses activities which can find their appropriate places in the curriculum and which contribute largely toward the accepted objectives of education.

Pilot Program of the Conservation Education Association

A long-range plan to codify, test, and make available a "model" program for state coordination of conservation education in the public schools has been developed by the Conservation Education Association and is now being tried out in the state of Washington. A preliminary step was the preparation of a theoretical plan assembled by a committee of Association members most familiar with existing problems and successful practices in a large number of the states. This dealt with teacher education, both in-service and pre-service, curricula materials, cooperation from agencies and resource people, the role of teacher-training institutions and state departments of education, the need for specialists at the state level, and similar concerns.

Next, an annual conference of the Association was devoted to testing the validity of the plan through analysis of the situation in selected states in comparison with the proposed model. Since the entire membership present participated in this process of evaluation and they represent trained personnel from almost every state, many refinements were achieved.

Finally, the state of Washington, supported with a small grant-in-aid, volunteered to field test the model plan by incorporating it with the existing program of conservation education in that state. It is the hope of the Association that this may start a process of sharing successful practices among many other states and will serve to implement chain reactions that will support and encourage existing programs and leadership.

American Camping Association

The American Camping Association is the professional organization representing all types of camping in the United States. It is concerned primarily with the expansion of camping opportunities and the improvement of camping practices. Many school outdoor education leaders are active in the American Camping Association, and the Association has established a national School Camping Committee to encourage school camp programs.

Through workshops and leadership training programs, the Association makes efforts to improve the leadership skills of camp leaders. In 1952 the Association conducted a national workshop on conservation in camping, from which there resulted a booklet, *Conservation in Camping,* which was published later by the Soil Conservation Service of the U.S. Department of Agriculture.

A grant of $5,000 a year for three years was made by the Lilly Foundation to the American Camping Association early in 1957. This grant is to be used to develop and expand programs in conservation education in camps.

American Institute of Park Executives

The American Institute of Park Executives and Michigan State University are co-operating in the publication of five technical bulletins on outdoor education. These publications are designed primarily for park administrators and others interested in planning outdoor education programs. The following publications are being prepared:

1. *Outdoor Education, a Way to Better Community Living.* This is a discussion of need for outdoor education in nature interpretation programs, types of programs, methods and techniques.

2. *School-Park Cooperation in Outdoor Education.* This is a consideration of school-park cooperation as a means of improving the programs of both organizations.

3. *Interpretative Programs, A Guide to Better Park Use.* This is a manual presenting essential information for setting up and conducting interpretative outdoor education programs in parks, camps, and similar areas.

4. *Improving Community Living Through Outdoor Beautification and Horticultural Programs.* This publication is designed to stimulate interest in community programs centered around home and neighborhood improvement.

5. *Nature Trail Labels.* This is a compilation of some 900 labels actually used on existing nature trails.

National Conference on State Parks

The National Conference on State Parks has been concerned for a number of years with the expansion of interpretive services to state park visitors. These services are intended to develop an understanding and appreciation on the part of the visitor of the scientific, historic, and scenic features of the particular park visited. In some states the interpretive services have been used extensively by school groups.

The Committee on Interpretation of the National Conference on State Parks has prepared material for parks relative to the organization and conducting of interpretive programs. The Conference has participated for three years in the conducting of a workshop for park naturalists and others interested in interpretive programs. The workshop has been held in cooperation with Indiana University and the American Institute of Park Executives. It has brought together each year about sixty people actively concerned with park interpretation.

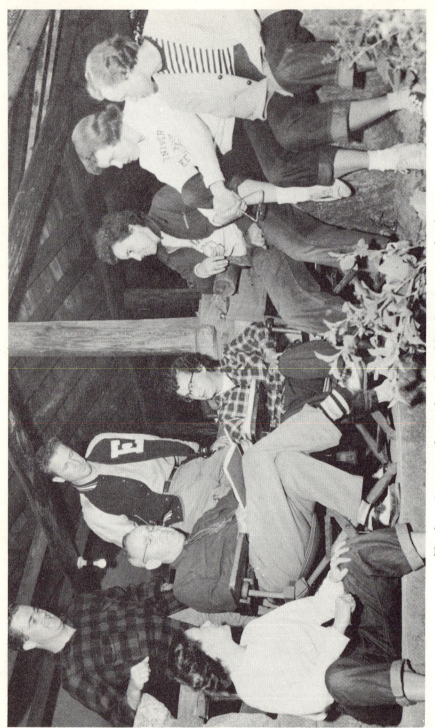

Teachers learn outdoor education skills in summer school camps.

CHAPTER IV

Teacher Preparation

1. Experiencing Reality in the Educational Process

MODERN life and modern education which prepares for life are moving further and further away from the kinds of basic experiences that make a person understand and appreciate the world in which he lives. It used to be that a youngster, as he grew up, would learn much about the immediate environment by being physically present when significant things were happening. He helped prepare the soil in the spring to receive the seed. He watched the seed drop into the ground. He tended the plant . . . saw it grow into maturity. He came to appreciate its importance to his own life. In the autumn the harvest had a special significance to him. The fruits of labor, the gift of the soil, man's preparation for the winter, all had a personal meaning.

A generation or two ago, many families had an intimate relation with animals. A cow, a horse, a pig, chickens, ducks, geese were common appendages to the household. Growing youngsters knew these animals, their needs, their life cycles, and their contribution to man's economic system.

In those days, the words which students in school read in their books had roots in reality. They reached back into the experiences which the youngster had as he grew to maturity. Today this is all quite different.

Extensive mobility has made it possible for the family to extend itself geographically. The child of today probably sees more of the surface of the earth than his father or grandfather did, but the acquaintance is not one of depth. For knowledge about the roots of things—for insight with depth of meaning, he must rely upon symbols or images. Sometimes it is the written word, sometimes a picture. Now it may be the talking, moving picture on the screen. These devices extend the breadth of vision, but they may not deepen the understanding. Unless these devices are supplemented by firsthand experience in depth, learning may still be surface knowledge with little opportunity for combining knowledge into related wholes.

Lack of Teacher Preparation

Because the modern child, especially the city child, does not have the opportunity to experience the things he is expected to learn about in their natural setting, his education often is artificial and lacks depth of meaning. Since the family no longer provides these experiences, the school and the teacher must do so as best they can.

But the school is terribly handicapped when trying to carry out this new responsibility. To begin with, the school room, with its walls and windows, is designed to keep the natural world out. Secondly, the school must run on a schedule and schedules do not lend themselves to natural explorations. Thirdly, and most important, teachers are not prepared to bring real experiences to children. Indeed many teachers have grown to maturity themselves without close contact with reality in the areas in which they are expected to teach.

There is little or nothing in the certification laws and regulations that require a teacher to have firsthand knowledge of his subject. Courses and credits based largely upon symbolic answers suffice to meet most certification requirements. The teacher learns from a book which was written by someone who read other books. The actual contact with reality is, therefore, far, far removed.

Examinations for course marks and credits are usually entirely verbal. An ability to respond to a written examination, based upon word symbols, usually has little relationship to basic, firsthand knowledge. Except in science education, this is almost universally true. And even some science education is amazingly unrealistic and remote from reality. In short, the stock in trade which many teachers have is knowledge and not wisdom or understanding.

Those who have ever worked with teachers, or young people preparing to be teachers, in a natural environment will testify as to their naivete about some of the basic facts of life about which they are expected to teach. Teachers who have verbalized about a subject for years, when confronted with the real thing, will not recognize it.

One advocate of outdoor education had a group of teachers on a walk one day when they came upon a field covered with luxuriant, golden growth. He asked the group if they knew what it was. None of them did. Reaching through the fence, he picked several stems and asked them to look closely and see if they could recognize them. Each one took a stem and examined it.

"It looks like a feather", one said.

"Part of a whisk-broom", another judged.

Still none of them recognized it. So the leader showed them how to crush it in their hands, blow away the chaff, and leave the golden kernels.

"Seed!", one of them discovered. But none of them knew yet what it was.

"Eat it!", the leader suggested.

They hesitatingly took the kernels in their mouths and chewed.

"What does it taste like?", they were asked.

"Puffed wheat!", one of them finally discovered.

All of their lives they had depended upon this product. They ate it in some form each day. They probably had taught about it time after time.

They had shown movies about it, assigned it as a topic for reports. But they did now know what it was when they saw it.

Disturbing Facts

This illustration is no isolated sample. Several years ago the writer prepared a list of questions about certain basic experiences. This questionnaire, known as a Reality Inventory, was distributed among hundreds of young people preparing to be teachers. There was no final grade, no pressure to answer one way or the other. The respondents did not sign their names. It was just an attempt to learn how extensive the firsthand experience of the respondents was. Some of the results were most amazing.

In a country with a pioneer tradition and an expansive outdoors in which to seek experience, it was surprising to find that forty-three per cent of the women and twenty-eight per cent of the men said they had never slept out-of-doors in their lives. Eleven per cent of the women and eight per cent of the men answered "no" to the query of whether they had ever made a fire outdoors. In a world where millions of people are undernourished, eighty-two per cent of the women and seventy-four per cent of the men said they had never been without food for twenty-four hours or more except when they were ill.

One out of eight of the women and one out of three of the men had never cooked a complete meal for two or more people in their lives, while sixty-two per cent of the men and fifty per cent of the women had never preserved or helped preserve fruit. More than a third of the men and nearly two thirds of the women said they had never walked ten miles or more at one time in their lives.

A Challenge to Teacher-Education Institutions

Can real depth of understanding and inspired teaching come from such backgrounds? This is a question that should be pondered carefully by those who prepare teachers. It may well be that a certain pattern of firsthand experience is just as important to the good teacher as a pattern of course credits.

To overcome this growing lack in our educational program, it is necessary to do two things. First, young people who are going into teaching as a profession should be given firsthand experiences about the things they expect to teach. Every program of teacher education should be carefully examined to see if the experience background of the candidates demands a systematic exposure to certain of the basic elements of the world in which they live.

Secondly, those who expect to be teachers should be introduced to the outdoors in such a way that they can and will provide experiences for the youngsters they will have under their care. Again, those who have worked with young teachers or those who are going to be teachers will testify that, once they have been introduced to outdoor education, they are likely to plan these kinds of experiences for the children they teach.

In addition to the teacher-education side of the problem, each community should consider the feasibility of providing facilities and resources that will make it possible for those teachers who wish to use the outdoors to do so without too much difficulty. Firsthand experience is important to modern education. It takes energy and ingenuity to provide these experiences. The average teacher will not do the job unless there is administrative and public support for her efforts.

2. Pre-Service Preparation

THE past decade has witnessed many new developments in teacher preparation for outdoor education. While it has been said by some that there is a lag between new programs and leadership training, this would not appear to be true concerning outdoor education. The following descriptions of pre-service and inservice preparation are only a few of many that could be reported throughout the United States. Those herein described have been chosen because they are representative geographically and include various sizes and types of colleges and universities. A number of others could be cited if time and space had permitted.

A State Program of Outdoor Education for Teachers

The New Jersey State School of Conservation, which has been in operation since the summer of 1949, is dedicated to: (1) providing educational experiences for students and teachers which will increase their appreciation for the importance of conservation in America today; (2) the training of future teachers and teachers in service in the use of the out-of-doors for educational purposes; and (3) conducting a demonstration children's camp utilizing conservation education as the main program feature.

The State School of Conservation was an idea in 1948. In 1949 it was launched in a modest way. During the season of 1956, it offered an extensive program which reached both adults and children.

The success of the New Jersey State School of Conservation can be attributed to a number of things, but certainly the excellent cooperation that has existed between the State Department of Educaion and the State Department of Conservation and Economic Development is a large factor. The Department of Conservation and Economic Development has been responsible for providing facilities and co-operating with the program, and the State Department of Education has developed and directed the program through the state teachers colleges.

Existing Camp Facilities Used

The facilities of the camp grew out of a Civilian Conservation Corps camp which was active in the late 1930s. The young men in this CCC camp, among other things, constructed some excellent facilities in the New Jersey Stokes State Forest. These facilities were designed for use as a summer camp by organizations desiring to rent them from the state.

The camp buildings constructed under this program were excellently designed. They consisted of a combination of native stone and timber construction and included a dining hall, an administration building, a recreation hall, an infirmary, a staff lodge, fourteen living cabins, and latrine and washroom facilities.

At the time the CCC program was terminated in the late '30s, the camp buildings were not quite completed; but they had progressed to a point where they were usable. The camp was used for a year or two by a council of social agencies in northern New Jersey and then lay idle for several years before the idea of a state school of conservation took shape.

Finances

When the plan to develop a state school of conservation was first proposed to the state legislature, it was based upon the assumption that the program would be almost entirely self-supporting. That is to say, that those who participated would, upon the payment of room, board, and tuition, provide the finances necessary to carry on the operation. The State of New Jersey, however, was to assume responsibility through the Department of Conservation and Economic Development for maintaining the physical facilities.

In order to organize and develop the program and launch it in the summer of 1949, the legislature appropriated $6,000. The Commissioner of Education requested that the New Jersey State Teachers College at Montclair assume responsibility for the administration of the camp, and the dean of the college was designated as the director. In this way, the New Jersey School of Conservation became a part of the part-time and extension division of the college and, as such, was empowered to offer courses for college credit under the administration of the college.

The Program

During the first summer, the program at the School of Conservation consisted of two undergraduate institutes in outdoor education and a series of graduate courses in conservation education, rural sociology, and field biology. After the first season's operation, it became evident that it would be advisable to establish a demonstration children's camp at the School of Conservation to serve two functions: (1) to provide demonstration opportunities in conservation education; and (2) to supplement the income and place the operation on a self-supporting basis. The children's camp was announced through the public schools and was an immediate success. Leadership for the camp was recruited from the faculties and students of the state teachers colleges, thereby providing experiences with children to the future teachers as well as supplying an excellent level of leadership for the camp.

The matter of recruiting participants for the graduate courses at the School of Conservation for teachers in service has never been easy due to summer commitments which provide income and the leisure to work toward graduate degrees. It has been difficult to fill the courses offered,

especially in the middle of the summer. There has been a tendency, therefore, for the graduate courses to be offered immediately after school
closes in the spring or just before school opens in the fall, with the summer
program for children occupying the middle part of the summer. However,
as teachers in conservation came to the School of Conservation and had
experiences in the out-of-doors, requests began to come in for the use of
the facilities for the school year by groups of school children. This has
been encouraged up to the point where such groups could be accom-
modated with the existing staff and facilities.

Extending the Program

It has been the policy of the school of Conservation to encourage outdoor education in communities in the state, but not to assume full responsibility once a program was established and moving under its own
power. The most successful community operation has been in Ridgewood, New Jersey, where the community has now established its own outdoor education program with professional leadership after having used
the facilities of the School of Conservation for a number of years. Because
of the program of the School of Conservation, a number of additional
communities began experimenting with outdoor education as a regular
part of the curriculum.

The value of outdoor experiences became apparent to all those participating in the program. It soon became evident that the extension of
these experiences to all students in teacher education would be a wise
move. The first move in this direction was to require all majors in science
education at the Montclair State Teachers College to complete a course
in field biology at the School of Conservation. Panzer College of Physical
Education has required two ten-day periods of camping experience of
all its undergraduates and has untilized the School of Conservation since
the school opened in the summer of 1949.

As the number of students from the state teachers colleges who participated in the School of Conservation program grew, it became increasingly evident that this was the kind of experience that all students
should have, especially those who grow up in a metropolitan area. The
presidents of the six state teachers colleges have consistently supported
this program in a variety of ways. Within the last year, this group has
officially endorsed, in principle, the idea that outdoor education experience should be provided for every student in the teachers colleges as
a regular part of the curriculum as soon as this is practical from the
standpoint of facilities and staff.

Plans for extension of the outdoor education program among all the
state teachers colleges have been drawn and it is hoped that further
moves in this direction can be made in the coming months to the extent
that resources will be available to provide these valuable experiences to
all students in teacher education.

Inter-disciplinary Approach for Preparing Teachers
and Leaders in Outdoor Education

University of California, Los Angeles

"Outdoor education" through general usage has grown to mean school camping in some educational circles. The major emphasis and activity directed toward this aspect of education has centered primarily at the elementary level. This occasions the concern that outdoor education may signify only elementary school camping to many educators. Actually, in its broadest context, it means far more than this. It refers to education in the out-of-doors at all age levels. It is broader than the specific skills involved in such outdoor activities as hunting, fishing, camping, hiking, star-gazing, rock collecting, bird-watching, skin-diving, canoeing, and boating. Actually, it is that phase of education which seeks to improve man's use of his physical environment for such activities. It implies first-hand contact with the out-of-doors and a study of the relationships of plants and animals to each other and to their environment, and the relationship of all these to man. It stresses the acquisition of knowledge and the development of understanding about the out-of-doors, based upon broad concepts and general principles rather than detailed facts. It presumes actual experiences in the out-of-doors in order that attitudes and appreciations can be developed that will result in improved behavior in terms of more intelligent use of the out-of-doors.

Outdoor education is not a new subject matter area. Rather, it is an interpretation of many subject matter areas through the use of the out-of-doors. In this sense it becomes a method of teaching—utilizing the out-of-doors as a laboratory for the purpose of interrelating a number of subjects which have been taught previously as separate unrelated courses or with minimum stress upon their interrelationships.

What the individual can learn about his physical environment will depend upon his age and previous experience. The nature of the outdoor education program should be adapted to the age level at which it is aimed. Outdoor education occurring at the secondary-school level should differ from that which occurs at the elementary-school level not only in terms of depth and scope of the subject matter covered at various age levels, but also in the manner by which it is interrelated.

In the early stages, organized camps and youth-serving and conservation agencies assumed responsibility for providing an environment for outdoor education. More recently, elementary schools, in an effort to supplement and enrich the regular school curriculum, have embraced camping. The common elements of these programs provide the basis for the development of a program of professional preparation of leadership for outdoor education. These common elements are: (1) science education, (2) conservation education, (3) social relationships, (4) recreation skills, (5) spiritual values, (6) personal health, and (7) democratic planning and participation.

Goals of Outdoor Education. Through urbanization, man has lost contact with his natural environment. Technology has led to an accelerated depletion of natural resources, while at the same time increasing the amount of man's leisure. Society is more dependent today upon the physical environment than ever before. Economically, society needs scientific experts in such areas as the conservation of soil, water, mineral, and other natural resources. Politically, society needs a citizenry well enough informed to support programs of conservation of these vital resources.

The development of common understandings and interests through outdoor education is one means of achieving these goals. The initial experience should be provided at the elementary-school level. However, outdoor education should not stop there. It is a lifelong process of such vital concern that it cannot be delegated to a single institution or agency in society. Today, such agencies as the National Park Service, the United States Forest Service, the Department of Agriculture (extension services through 4-H clubs, farm organizations, *etc.*), the Fish and Wildlife Service, various state agencies concerned with conservation, as well as schools and organized camps stress the importance of and conduct programs of outdoor education for all age levels.

As is often the case, the leaders now in the field are pioneers. They have blazed the trail, so to speak, before professional education has really organized to prepare leaders for outdoor education. School districts currently require the regular teaching credential of those persons conducting outdoor education programs. The credential categories include the school camp teacher-counselor, the school camp administrator, the outdoor education supervisor, and the conservation supervisor. In some instances, the science and art supervisors are pressed into service. Federal, state, and county agencies other than schools do not require the credentials although leaders in these agencies have functions similar to those of school personnel. In this group are conservation educators, consultants and coordinators of outdoor education, and ranger park naturalists. In the field of organized camping, private camps and youth-serving agencies with camping programs employ personnel in similar capacities.

Desired Leadership Competencies. The services rendered by these leaders have assumed several specialized forms. For example, many outdoor educators have direct teaching relationship with participants of various age levels. Others may be responsible for administrative and organizational functions with particular emphasis upon the promotion, planning, and coordination of programs. Some specialists work with participants as individuals, others work with people in groups. However, through all of these run the common threads of: (1) the ability to understand science and its interrelationships, and (2) the ability to present these concepts to other people. In essence, *the ideal outdoor educator possesses a broad scientific background with a firm grasp of the meaning and significance of this background in relationship to his physical en-*

*vironment; he possesses the ability to communicate this in socially signifi-
cant terms to others.*

In only a few isolated situations has academic education been organized to provide this level of professional preparation. The majority of
leaders now in the field have had to supplement their backgrounds
through experience and in-service education. In this sense, they have
pioneered not only today's program, but also the general framework for
the preparation of tomorrow's leadership. It is from the results of their
experimental approaches to the design of outdoor education programs
that teacher-education institution should determine the nature of the
desired preparation. At the present time, it appears that this preparation
should provide the potential outdoor educator with an understanding
of his physical environment, himself, and his relationship to society. In
addition, he should have opportunity to: (1) develop understandings,
knowledges, and skills related to working with people in the teaching
situation, (2) develop skills in the program activities normally found in
the outdoor education environment, and (3) integrate all of these through
intensive field-work experiences. The section of the diagram appearing on
page 118, labeled "Nature of the Desired Preparation", is an effort to
depict the various areas which can and should contribute to the preparation of outdoor educators and may be more descriptive than written
treatment of this aspect.

The Inter-disciplinary Approach—As the diagram suggests, this professional preparation cannot be provided within a single department or college in an educational institution. The institutional pattern of preparation should reflect the same flexibility and creativity as the experimental
approach employed in the field. The university setting appears to lend
itself particularly well to this concept. The university, composed of
separate schools and colleges such as agriculture, education, letters and
science, applied arts, social group work, and augmented by rich resources
in staff, students, physical facilities, (laboratories, libraries, *etc.*), research
programs, and experimental programs, is equipped to provide the preparation outlined above.

There are several ways in which this preparation can be approached
at the university level. However, one method which affords several advantages and appears conducive to "best" preparation is called the "inter-
disciplinary approach."

In brief, the inter-disciplinary approach is an attempt to utilize those
resources of the total university which can contribute to the preparation
desired. The term implies the coordination of the offerings of many
disciplines and departments through a single department vested with administrative responsibilities and assuming the role of "coordinating department." Some of the disciplines and departments that can contribute
to the program are: botany, biology, zoology, astronomy, geology,
anthropology, psychology, education, physical education, recreation,

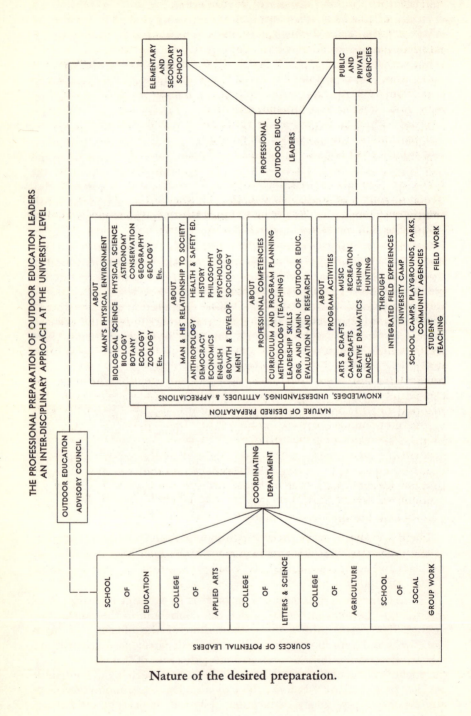

THE PROFESSIONAL PREPARATION OF OUTDOOR EDUCATION LEADERS
AN INTER-DISCIPLINARY APPROACH AT THE UNIVERSITY LEVEL

Nature of the desired preparation.

sociology, art, music, and theater arts. Several of the advantages which this approach affords are: (1) duplication of courses, staff, and facilities is avoided; (2) students in the program are exposed to the professional ideas, perspectives, and knowledges of specialists in these disciplines; (3) students can enter the program from many areas; (4) concern for the program is shared by many participating departments; (5) students have opportunity to explore a wide range of offerings; and (6) preparation can be creative by matching the program to the individual's needs, interests, and goals.

The Advisory Council. The preceding diagram illustrates how the resources of a university could be organized for the inter-disciplinary approach. Interested students in the several schools and colleges of the university participate in the preparation program through the coordinating department. An advisory council, composed of representatives from those departments directly concerned with the preparation of outdoor education leaders, resource representatives from other departments, and lay professionals from community agencies operating outdoor education programs, serves to guide and implement the inter-disciplinary approach. Some of the functions of this council are: (1) to serve in an advisory capacity in the planning and guiding of the program of professional preparation of outdoor education leadership; (2) to inform departments, schools, and colleges in the university of trends, needs, plans, and developments in the field of outdoor education as they emerge; (3) to serve as a medium for stimulating departments to analyze and evaluate their courses and experiences as resources for students in outdoor education; (4) to render advisory service relative to outdoor education to interested school districts, educational agencies, organizations, workshops, and the like; and (5) to interpret the concepts and purposes of the outdoor education program and the functions of the council to the university and the community.

As examples, two items which the advisory council might consider in fulfilling these functions are: (1) Should the university operate a camp?; and (2) How can the university help integrate the outdoor education point of view in existing state and local courses of study?

Important Considerations. The responsibility for planning and developing the over-all program and the organization and leadership of the advisory council is delegated to a "coordinating department" by the university administration. It should be apparent from the foregoing discussion and the diagram that any of several departments could assume the role of coordinator. Traditionally, camping has been taught in departments of physical education or recreation. Because of the close relationship of camping to outdoor education, there is some rationale for centering such education in physical education or recreation departments. Due to credential requirements and the emphasis on school camping, the school of education might be the logical coordinating unit. However, because of the importance of science and conservation, one of the biological science departments might be so designated. Each educational institution should decide for itself where responsibility for the coordination of the outdoor education program best belongs. This decision should be based upon the local situation and should ensure that the full resources of the institution are utilized.

The nature of the desired preparation was previously identified by means of the diagram in terms of five general areas essential to the preparation of outdoor education leaders. A student would not take all of the subject areas courses indicated. Rather, he would supplement his existing background and experience with knowledges, appreciations, attitudes, and understandings in the five general areas in the light of his professional goals. The nature of the desired preparation has consciously been expanded to emphasize the breadth and scope of university offerings. Although compartmentalized in the diagram, this is done for graphic purposes and the dotted line indicates how these areas are co-related to the total program through the advisory council.

Full use should be made of community resources in the preparation program. This is made possible through such avenues as membership on the advisory council, utilization of professionals from the field as instructors and lecturers, and use of operating programs for supervised field-work experiences.

For the potential outdoor education leader who envisions a career in the schools, opportunity should be provided for meeting the proper credential requirements. To those students seeking leadership opportunities in outdoor education in other public and private agencies, an avenue should be provided leading to the non-credential positions of park naturalists, consultant in outdoor education, camp administrator, *etc.* Certain elements of teacher education are necessary for all outdoor education leaders. The delineation made in the chart merely indicates that, in terms of employment, it may be necessary to meet specific requirements for the credential and that specialized courses may be necessary. Since employment patterns are not clearly defined, the program of professional preparation should be flexible and opportunity should exist to adapt the institutional pattern to the emerging demands and needs of the field.

The approach presented is one which is being experimented with in several institutions throughout the country. Additional institutions may see fit further to implement or explore this method and to experiment with modifications and adaptations of the concept of an inter-disciplinary approach at the university level. Certainly the goals and objectives of outdoor education merit the concern and best efforts of all education.

Michigan State University

While all elementary and many secondary-school teachers should be able to teach in the out-of-doors, there is a need for some to have more intensive preparation for positions of leadership in outdoor education in schools and colleges. Based on the thesis that outdoor education is neither a subject matter field nor a separate discipline, but is a way of teaching and a climate for learning, all appropriate departments, divisions, and schools in a college or university should be involved in setting up a curriculum for outdoor education.

The essentials in a program for leadership in outdoor education should include an understanding of human growth and development and the learning process, the ability to interpret the outdoors as a learning laboratory, techniques and understandings needed in teaching in an informal outdoor setting, and skills and appreciations for enjoying the outdoors. The courses and experiences needed to achieve these competencies would involve education, the physical and social sciences, conservation, sociology, social work, *etc.* Consequently, at the graduate level, especially, it would be necessary to tailor the offerings in outdoor education in accordance with the training and experience of the individual.

An example of this approach will be found at Michigan State University where outdoor education is considered an area of emphasis. The course work and activities related to outdoor education are interwoven into the candidate's major field. For example, a student with an undergraduate background of science would need more of his graduate experiences in education, such as educational psychology, child growth and development, and physical education. Similarly, a student majoring in the field of physical education would require more work in science, conservation, and general education courses. All would need field experiences in camps and other outdoor settings. A few special courses combining an interpretation of the outdoors, teaching techniques, and patterns of outdoor education should be provided, preferably through courses of a workshop nature. Such is the case at Michigan State University College of Education where off-campus courses in outdoor education and a three-week summer workshop are conducted for pre-service and in-service preparation of teachers and leaders.

The inter-disciplinary pattern for outdoor education, therefore, implies that all the appropriate offerings on a campus should be included in planning a series of experiences that will help all teachers and others interested to make the best use of the outdoors for learning. Wherever possible, existing courses in the various disciplines can be adapted to meet the growing trend for teacher preparation for outdoor education. A minimum number of new courses should be added, as needed, by the appropriate departments. A campus committee, made up of representatives of all divisions and departments involved, should be designated to plan the offerings in outdoor education. Camps and other outdoor settings should be used for field experiences, internships, and student teaching.

One of the best plans for student teaching is the use of selected communities where students live and teach for a term or semester. The centers selected have school camping and other types of outdoor programs so that prospective teachers may have an opportunity to participate in classroom related outdoor experiences in a broad educational curriculum. Such is the situation at Michigan State University where several of the student-teacher centers have school camping, school forests, and gardening programs in the curriculum.

This approach to teacher and leadership preparation is consistent with the broad interpretation of outdoor education described in this book and is the best assurance that the outdoors will have maximum use in providing better educational experiences for children and youth.

Internships in Outdoor Education

Antioch College

In Ohio, a short distance from the urban centers of Fairborn, Xenia, Springfield, and Dayton, on virtually an island of natural wooded land, the Antioch College Outdoor Education Center has just started a much-needed and rapidly expanding program. The first two objectives of the program are concerned with: (1) demonstrating land-use management in the devolpment of a natural area for outdoor education, and (2) providing school camping experiences for elementary school children within a sixty-mile radius of the camp. The third objective, and most relevant to this article, is to provide, using the Outdoor Education Center as headquarters, for leadership training and experience in outdoor education for: (1) college students majoring in elementary education and natural science; (2) in-service school personnel; and (3) pre-and in-service personnel of private and public programs concerned with camping and the out-of-doors.

Administrators are becoming more interested in knowing that the personnel they employ as teachers of the fifth and sixth grades, teachers of science, and instructors in the natural sciences at the college level have experience and training in using the out-of-doors as an enhancement to learning. The utilization of internships for the undergraduate or graduate student, and workshops, seminars, conventions, *etc.* for the in-service personnel should be forth-coming.

Among the finer education opportunities which exist in the program of the new Center at Antioch are the two or three internships offered to graduates or undergraduates who can arrange to receive credit for a form of apprentice education. Many training institutions already make these arrangements for their practice-teaching experiences. Outdoor education internships need to be utilized in a similar fashion, both for elementary education majors and majors in the natural sciences. The Antioch College Center is only a newcomer among the many programs about the country that are qualified and interested in offering such "learning by doing" experiences for qualified students.

Antioch students interested in internships in outdoor education, in addition to their opportunities on the campus, can work with: (1) school camping in California, Michigan, New York, New Hampshire, or Ohio; (2) the nature-counselor phase of private and public summer and day camps; (3) children's and natural-history museums; (4) governmental agencies such as the United States Departments of Agriculture, Interior, and Natural Resources, and the United States Geological Survey in a variety of jobs: (5) the Marine Biological Laboratories in California or Massachusetts; (6) an observatory staff; or (7) the National Parks.

While some of these internships can be arranged only through a work-study plan such as Antioch maintains, those in school camps about the country would be, and have been, particularly ideal for other colleges or universities. The realization that leadership training for outdoor education, like outdoor education itself, is best accomplished "in the field" with all the motivation and gratification of spontaneity and non-simulated problem solving, needs applause and action-support in addition to lip service.

Springfield College

Eligibility for an internship at Springfield College is initially earned by successfully completing instruction in the following courses, or being able to evidence the equivalence of such experience: (1) introduction to camp leadership, conservation, physical science; (2) introductory courses in arts and crafts, music, dramatics, first aid; (3) primary skills and techniques in games and sports for playground, gymnasium, field, and court; boating and canoeing; swimming, diving, and lifesaving; and (4) fundamentals in rhythms, folk and square dances. It should be understood that these courses are not considered to be ends unto themselves. Rather, their value exists to serve as sources. Also, the content, when selected, should be determined on the basis of functional use in camp settings for children.

Active trainee participation attempts to develop a recognition and an acceptance of four personal-development goals: (1) exposure; (2) experience; (3) experimentation; and (4) evaluation. Students who earn eligibility for outdoor education and school camping are usually quick to see these relationships. Thus these goals become not only the curriculum design, but also the goals of each student when he or she enrolls for the ten-week internship with some school camp. Some students, however, prefer to attend special visitations to local school systems for a week or more at a time, such as Newton, Massachusetts, or the Boston University Sargent Camp in New Hampshire, or the newly established outdoor education program at Ridgewood, New Jersey. However, over the years since 1946, Springfield College students have served in school camping block placements in the states of California, Michigan, Texas, New Jersey, New Hampshire, and Massachusetts.

A three-way problem exists and must be solved by all three personalities working hand in hand—the trainee, the college adviser, and the school camp director-supervisor. When a placement is located, involvement is reduced to two basic parts.

Part One includes the matter of relating the trainee first to the selection of and the necessary arrangements for a block placement with a qualified school camp or outdoor education director. Second, the process calls for a written job description of the responsibilities of the trainee by the school camp director. It is deemed important that all three parties concerned be involved with the changes, or acceptance and final approval of such a statement. A third step calls for what Dr. Jay B. Nash used to identify as "teachable moments." These are the many personal matters which must be accomplished by the trainee. In short, these include budgeting of finances, food, housing, travel, college registration, and so forth. Extreme care should be taken by the college adviser at this juncture to assure that a block placement does not become a financially remunerative experience, but rather an educational experience for which "expenses," at best, may be received by the trainee. Also, selection would assume that the director-supervisor would not misuse or make money on trainees. Expenses at best, then, is the neutral goal for all concerned. A fourth step for the college adviser also becomes the first step for awareness of and supervision by the school camp director.

This fourth and transition step involves trainees' records and reports. Here, however, the trainee must initiate full responsibility to develop some system of a daily log or diary of exposures, experiences, and experiments, all of which must be later evaluated. To assist with this process and to help the trainee to keep on target, a weekly report letter is sent by the trainee to the college adviser, and a copy is provided the school camp director. At half time (5 weeks), a progress report letter is prepared. A summary of reports to date, guided by the original job description and by the four goals identified above, is expected. This permits opportunity for the trainee to identify those things which have been left undone, as well as to give perspective and priority to those things that should be attempted during the last half of the block placement period. Lastly, a final report is completed which should have the benefit of consultation by the trainee with the school camp director and with the college adviser.

Part Two delineates the reality of the school camp setting. The school camp setting, as expected and planned in the job description mentioned above, should provide for *at least* the following opportunities:

First, the trainee is to be directly *exposed* to the realities of responsibilities with children away from home. The trainee shall be assigned to live in a camp shelter with a group of children and will be held responsible for their health and safety as well as for their growth and development. The trainee should expect to eat at the same table with the children. He will want to play and learn with the children. To accomplish such exposure, the trainee will serve under the school camp director and will assist either the home-room teacher or another specialist on the staff, or will lead a variety of groups or classes in activity that has been previously planned by the home-room teacher, the school camp director, and/or the children. In short, the trainee serves in multiple roles as counselor, leader, teacher, friend, adviser, and enabler.

Second, the trainee should gain *experience* with some of the basic demands often made upon teacher-leaders. Thus the trainee's observations will include many individuals motivated by curiosity and interest, or fear and insecurity, in a myriad of things in the out-of-doors school-camp setting. In addition, numerous social and political facets of group life will seek dominance. Experience reveals that human problems will prevail, and lessons in the need for human independence, dependence, and interdependence will most likely abound in such settings, often testing a "Solomon." The influence of attitudes and the impact of behavioral practices are normal and natural to such basic learnings in a camp setting. Scheduled and unscheduled knowledge areas and needs often loom large in these dynamic settings. Adaptability and the invaluable skills and techniques mastered back at college will now show up in dramatic and sometimes embarrassing moments. These essential experiences are "grist for the mill" in one's internship.

A third opportunity should provide for trainee *experimentation* with the solving of problems under the expert eye and the guiding spirit of the qualified school camp director.

The fourth opportunity essential to the school camp internship is to expect, as well as to understand, the demands of, and the need for *evaluations.* With these each trainee must wrestle.

Trainees who have proved successful to themselves and to others have taught the writer that the Springfield College internship demands at least three objectives. Trainees are to: (1) earn eligibility for an internship; (2) strive for the goals of *exposure* to many ideas and persons in a successful school camp setting under top caliber leadership; to seek multiple *experiences* with children and teachers as individuals and in small group settings; to *experiment* whenever and wherever possible but always under clinical guidance of a supervisor; and to *evaluate,* always in a search for meaning and value of activity performed by humans; and (3) seek and develop self-imposed disciplines that are concerned with attitudes, concepts, knowledges and skills—these appear to lead to competence.

State University of New York Teachers College, Cortland

All students majoring in the four-year undergraduate professional training curriculum in recreation education are required to complete satisfactorily a full semester of field-work experience off campus for which they get a total of sixteen semester hours credit. This field work requirement consists of two different kinds of experiences at two different places for a minimum period of eight weeks each. All students are assigned one eight-week period serving in a public recreation program within the state of New York. The student, subject to final approval by the recreation education department of the college, may choose the area of field work in which he wishes to engage for the other eight-week period. Elective areas include school camping, youth-serving agencies, industrial recreation, and hospital recreation. Each year since 1952, from four to six juniors in recreation education at Cortland have chosen to do a part of their field work in school camping. The school camps training them include Clear Lake Camp in Michigan; Camp Cuyamaca in San Diego, California; Norwalk, California, School Camps; and Boston University Sargent Camp in Peterborough, New Hampshire.

Field Experience in School Camping

An effective teacher leads from courage rather than from fear. She is guided largely by the purposes of children rather than from those of adults. She "plays it by ear" and leads toward the child-centered goal rather than from the stereotypes of her society. Where, in our American culture, can she gain this courage to perform effectively? Certainly not from reading books and listening to lectures, or from practicing in the classroom, controlled as it is, by cultural stereotypes and cliches as well as by adult-planned courses of study. In fact, our highly organized society presents few opportunities whereby a student teacher can get experience with a group of children in a "free" situation. The school camp can provide this opportunity and is gaining in favor as a training locale for teachers and other group leaders. To a lesser degree, school farms and social-recreational programs provide similar conditions.

The essential elements which make leadership training in the school camp different from the classroom are:

(1) It is a 24-hour, round-the-clock type of experience.

(2) Children are away from home and away from school and usually check their inhibitions before arrival.

(3) The genuine workshop method can be employed.

(4) All learning situations are complete. Choosing a project, setting purposes, planning to carry them out, organizing committees, carrying out the project, and evaluation makes a complete learning experience. In one week at camp, twelve complete learning situations can occur whereas in the average classroom not that many units are completed in a year's time. Evaluation can be in terms of "how well did we do with our plans" rather than "how much content did we learn." Leaders can see the relationship between planning and the results, a function rather obscure in most schoolrooms.

(5) The false assumption that the teacher must know the content and the answers before she can be an effective teacher can be disproved in camp. Through actual practice, teachers can get an inner feeling for the fine art of instruction vs. entertainment— of placing a question back to the inquirer for his own research.

(6) Most camp activities are functional. This makes it a practical laboratory to experiment with various approaches to teaching— teacher-imposed plans vs. teacher-camper plans. Busy work, as such, is obnoxious.

(7) The camp program gives a teacher a sense of that undefined line where at one time she operates completely at the child's level and at another she becomes the status person. Most classrooms require the teacher to maintain her status at all times.

(8) In camp, the leader can learn from mistakes since bad practice is not as costly as in the classroom.

Battle Creek (Clear Lake) Public School Camp

The importance of camp experience in training teachers and group leaders has long been known by Michigan colleges of education. Recently, however, it has become an optional requisite in the larger institutions with staff personnel appointed to coordinate the effort.

The Clear Lake Camp experiment in teacher training began in September 1952 with several state-supported institutions participating. A year later, the faculty of Western Michigan College made it possible for juniors to spend a week at camp. In late 1954, the School of Education of Michigan State University opened a student-teacher center in Battle Creek. One of the requirements of the program compelled each participant to spend a week working in the school camp program. During the summer of 1956, a two-week experience at Clear Lake Camp was made a requirement for credit in student teaching. This current year, approximately 130 students from Michigan State University will have experience at Clear Lake Camp as a partial requirement of their student-teaching program.

The program is still emerging and will no doubt take on many new forms in the future. Some of the criteria which seem to guide the effort at present are:

(1) That students should come to camp for the sole purpose of seeing and learning about "kids." The camp cannot take them as a form of inexpensive labor.

(2) The camp director and staff must be competent teachers and have the skills to help student teachers find "better ways."

(3) Students should have staff status and should arrive in camp several hours ahead of the children.

(4) The camp director and staff should hold several discussion-conferences with students during the week for the purpose of identifying problems of leadership and interpreting clues of strategy.

(5) The camp director should hold a final evaluation conference with each student on "how does he feel" about his relations with children? with his peers? with teaching in general? What kinds of children does he like best? What leadership problems gave him the greatest trouble?

Of all the student teachers in training who have participated in the Clear Lake Camp experiment, two out of three had never had a prior experience with a group of children. Couple this with the fact that their only experience before graduation will come in a formal classroom, a place often devoid of any child-centeredness, it becomes obvious why Michigan State University and other Michigan teachers colleges have put a high priority on camp experience for their student teachers. This is especially true of secondary teachers who often go directly into a subject-centered classroom without ever having had a child-centered experience. There is substantial evidence that a camp experience will give a teacher the courage to be an effective leader.

Northern Illinois State College

A unique program in teacher education is in effect at Northern Illinois State College at DeKalb. All students majoring in elementary education are involved in three successive outdoor-education experiences at the Lorado Taft Field Campus in Oregon, Illinois. Because of the education department's block setup in which students meet with one instructor for a block of time varying from two to four hours a day, it is possible for students to spend considerable time in class planning and preparing for the field experience in outdoor education.

The first of these experiences takes place during the sophomore block when students spend a two-and-one-half-day period at the field campus exploring the concept of the out-of-doors as a laboratory for learning. This initial exposure of outdoor education is an attempt to develop an awareness to the out-of-doors as an extension of the classroom. The primary focus is upon analyzing the nature of the learning process by having students examine closely their own reactions as learners when confronted with new learning situations.

During the junior year, students are involved at the Field Campus for three days. This time, the emphasis is upon investigating various subject matter areas of the elementary curriculum and searching for ways of enriching and supplementing these content areas by means of firsthand observations and direct experiences. The culminating experience in outdoor education occurs when seniors return to spend a full week of school camping, living with and teaching a class of elementary pupils.

Prior to the actual week of school camping, seniors spend time setting up their own objectives, familiarizing themselves with the school-camp routine, and preparing for the learning activities which they will be called upon to teach. In most cases this professional preparation by college students also includes periodic visits to the sixth-grade classroom with which they will be working. During these visits, college students assist the children in planning for the kinds of activities which they want to carry out, and help direct the pupils' thinking in terms of establishing purposes for these learning activities.

During the week of school camping, in addition to teaching children in the out-of-doors, college students also assume responsibility for supervising children in the dining hall, teaching a singing grace, supervising the rest period, supervising the camp store, putting children to bed, and song leading. College students also take an active role in helping children evaluate daily the kinds of learning which are taking place. They very often keep anecdotal records and do sociometric studies which will increase their own understanding of children. In most cases, the college students pay a visit to the sixth-grade class upon their return to school in order to see the kinds of follow-up activities which have resulted from the week of school camping.

By the time a student majoring in elementary education is graduated, he has been exposed to three successive and related experiences in outdoor education at the Field Campus. It is believed that these students will be more effective teachers for having the knowledges and skills which will enable them to take their own pupils into the larger classroom of the out-of-doors and use it as an effective teaching medium.

Southern Illinois University

For the past seven years, Southern Illinois University has included outdoor education as an integral part of its higher education program. Subscribing to the educational principle that people learn by doing and that information when actually experienced is more meaningful and the individual will retain it longer, the Recreation and Outdoor Education Department, in cooperation with the teacher education program of the College of Education, provides many opportunities for students to "learn while living" out-of-doors.

There are three main avenues through which experiences may be gained in outdoor education. The University School offers prospective teachers an opportunity to observe and participate in a five-day school camping program for eighth-grade children. The local public schools and other elementary schools from neighboring communities participate annually in school camping. The University Camp, operated by the Recreation and Outdoor Education Department, also includes training in outdoor education for those interested during the summer months.

Up to this time, the University School and the public schools were either using Giant City State Park (12 miles from Carbondale) or the University Camp (located on Grassy Lake ten miles from the main campus). Now all schools in Southern Illinois (southern 31 counties) interested in school camping can utilize a central area (eventually 1400 acres) set aside by the Educational Council of 100 for Outdoor Education.

The University School's camping program is held during the last part of May, but the planning for curriculum and the mechanics for administering such a school camp are started early in the year. Many meetings are held for coordinating all the various subject areas, and all the teachers, staff members, and resource personnel are brought together to review and evaluate the previous year's camping program.

There are many reasons why this program is thoroughly planned in advance, but one particularly important reason is that the curriculum within the school must be planned and timed in such a way as to include school camping in a logical sequence—thus, the students are ready for what is coming and the experience is much more meaningful to them! Another important factor is that the prospective teachers doing practice teaching have an opportunity to see the entire curriculum progression and the relationship between theory and practice—to put it another way, to see those things which can be best taught in the classroom and to see how those things are taught which can be best taught in the out-of-doors.

Each summer the Recreation and Outdoor Education Department offers courses for credit at the University Camp. Last year, there were 125 undergraduate and graduate students (coed) registered for four to twelve units of credit during the eight-week camping season. This year, there are eleven different departments offering courses appropriate in the out-of-doors. Among the various courses offered are several that provide desirable field experience in outdoor education. Students may register for four quarter units of practice teaching, four quarter units in school camping and outdoor education programs, four quarter units in geographic bases of outdoor education, and two to eight quarter units in a graduate workshop in outdoor education.

Students from any department within the University are welcome to visit and observe the outdoor education program in action—in fact, during the actual camping period (whether it is in spring or summer), many students, freshmen to seniors, and teachers from area schools take the opportunity to see this "doing" program. However, the ones who receive the greatest benefits are those who live, work, play, and learn with the campers. Prospective teachers and future recreation leaders discover that these school camping programs provide an unequalled opportunity and one of the richest experiences they have during their educational career. It is our hope that with the central camp area for outdoor education, all teachers will, in the near future, have the chance to participate in a school camping program and receive credit as part of their total field-work experience.

Recommendations from the 1957 National Conference on Professional Preparation of Recreation Personnel

There is now in the United States an organized camping movement with some fourteen thousand camps and over four million five hundred thousand children. The rising tide of interest in outdoor education involving camp experiences, field trips, farm and garden programs, and travel experiences may soon become a major aspect of the public school program. The interest of park and recreation departments and forestry agencies in wise and proper use of their resources constitutes another large segment of society interested in outdoor education. The growing and varied outdoor pursuits is indicative of the need for consideration of expanded concern for trained leadership.

There is an increasing field for full-time professional personnel in camping outdoor education, and with agencies administering public lands. Increasingly, positions like these will need to be filled by individuals with special competence. For these people some specialized graduate training is needed. In addition to people in the full-time professional field, there is an increasing number of part-time or summer positions. This is particularly evident in the over two hundred thousand camp personnel now serving in summer camps who need help in improving their leadership skills.

Because of the diversity of interest in the outdoor education and camping field, there is some question at this time as to whether a curriculum should be developed encompassing the whole field. Only time will determine whether a different emphasis may be needed.

It is recognized that in a very few cases, probably on a regional level, institutions of higher learning may have a special curriculum in camp administration. In outdoor education, areas of emphasis might be set up as part of the Master's degree in recreation, teacher education, natural resources, or other related fields.

Some Guiding Principles

Whether a camp administration curriculum, or an area of emphasis in outdoor education, is the pattern developed in a particular school the following principles are pertinent:

1. Only those institutions of higher education with proper outdoor areas, staff, and other resources should give such a special program.
2. The needs for professional training in a particular locale will also be a determining factor.
3. An important part of the training program should be in an outdoor setting. Opportunity in the out-of-doors should include field experiences and observation.
4. Since outdoor education is an intra-discipline field, the various resources of the institution should be called upon. These might include conservation, science, forestry, music, arts and crafts, and those other resources related to the outdoor education program.

Uniqueness of the Camping Program

Camping and outdoor education requires certain leadership and administrative skills different in a large part from either general recreation or the traditional school program. The following are some of the characteristics of camping and outdoor education:

1. Education takes place in an informal setting generally in small groups.
2. Learning is largely through direct experiences.
3. The close personal relationship between leader and learner is making possible effective guidance and counseling to meet individual needs of participants.

4. Much of the program is related to the natural environment, which requires special skills and knowledges.

Content Areas for the Camping Specialization

In the field of camping administration, certain knowledges and skills are essential. It is assumed that people in this field will assume certain responsibilities for directing and supervision on the administrative level. The following areas should be included:

Administration of camps (finances, selection and supervision of staff, health and safety, facility development, management, *etc.*)

Program (program construction)

Child growth and development

Research methods

Philosophy of camping and outdoor education

Direct experience and field experience

And others as indicated by needs of individuals.

The field of outdoor education is less clearly defined than camping administration. Content in an area of experience will vary from institution to institution depending on such factors as local needs, staff resources, and cooperation of staff members from other disciplines. The following emphases might be considered:

1. Adopting the administrative structure in classroom procedures, for use of the natural environment.
2. Integrating subject matter content with outdoor experiences.
3. Developing knowledge of available community resources for outdoor education.

3. IN-SERVICE PREPARATION

Local Workshops

Dearborn Public Schools

THE Dearborn Public Schools in cooperation with Eastern Michigan College conducts two in-service training workshops each year for classroom teachers, resource personnel, and college students who are involved in the year-round school camping program. The three-week workshops are held at the beginning of the first and second semesters, and the teachers who will have classrooms at camp during the school year have a camping and training experience in preparation for the school program.

The workshop participants actually go through the program activities in the same way as is done by the school campers. This includes camp living, hikes and trips, conservation projects, program planning, and evaluation. The careful planning done by classroom teachers, camp staff college instructors, interns, conservation personnel, and other resource leaders is reflected in the quality of the Dearborn outdoor school program.

A unique phase of the entire program is the affiliation with several teacher preparation institutions including Eastern Michigan College, Michigan State University, Antioch College, Springfield College, and others whereby field experiences in outdoor education are combined with school camping. Many prospective teachers have periods in the school camp varying from one to twelve weeks.

A graduate off-campus course in outdoor education sponsored by Eastern Michigan College and the Dearborn Schools is another example of in-service training. The class meets at the camp one evening a week throughout a semester which adds realism to the course. Plans are underway for a summer session in outdoor education. This will be held at Mill Lake State Group Camp, located in a state recreation area of 14,000 acres where the Dearborn Outdoor School is now being conducted.

Minneapolis Public Schools

One of the richest, yet most inexpensive laboratories for all fields of education, but used the least, is the out-of-doors. It is understandable, for many teachers were taught to handle classes indoors and from materials learned from books and, therefore, feel ill at ease at the thought of moving outside. To be of assistance to teachers, Minneapolis has an Outdoor Education Committee, composed of elementary, junior high-school and senior high-school teachers, principals, lay members, and a consultant appointed by the superintendent of schools. The Committee serves a three-year term and meets once a month. The purpose of this Committee is to stimulate an interest in and appreciation of the values of outdoor education in the community.

Specific objectives are: (1) to help teachers discover the things which can best be taught in the out-of-doors; (2) to suggest, develop, and illustrate methods and techniques for use in outdoor education; and (3) to locate, acquaint, and assist teachers in the use of resources in outdoor education. Emphasis in all activities is placed upon active participation, and teachers discover that it is not necessary to know all the answers; that it is possible for a class and teacher to discover and learn together.

Weekends in a camp, planned for teachers by the Outdoor Education Committee, offer one of the best means for opening up the possibilities of learning in the out-of-doors. By starting out after school on Friday and closing by 4:00 P.M. on Saturday, it gives teachers the feeling that there is still time left for themselves. An informal atmosphere breaks down barriers, and with teachers from all grade levels, principals, consultants, and assistant superintendents present, there is opportunity to get acquainted and appreciate one another in a way which is sometimes difficult in large-city systems.

Friday evening introduces the group to fun activities at the table at dinner time, followed by mixers and games which help one relax, know people better, and just have fun. The evening campfire is a time for songs, inspiration, and learning a bit about what is to follow on Saturday. Saturday starts out with small groups going off to cook breakfast for themselves. In the morning, various explorations are provided whereby one group might discover a hidden lake and try to find out the evidences of the glacial period; another group might visit the foundation of an abandoned farm and attempt to reconstruct the history of the farm and the community of one hundred years ago. These groups are learning how to see, hear, feel, and to figure out answers to questions for themselves.

In the afternoon, there is an opportunity to make things out of the native materials they might have discovered on their morning trips, so that everyone goes home with something he has made—corn-husk mats, pins, birch candle holders, wall placques out of grasses, or polished stones. Such weekends in the fall, winter, or spring help teachers appreciate and feel comfortable in the outdoors and see the rich opportunities offered with each season.

An after-school in-service program limited to twenty-four teachers, in which the teachers plan with the Outdoor Education Committee the activities that would be most meaningful to them, is valuable from the standpoint of teachers from kindergarten through high school working together and each one getting help so that a class will benefit from the teacher's experiences. Activities that this group participated in consisted of what could be done on the steps of the schools in a five- or ten-minute period, on the school grounds, within the block, or at a nearby city park, covering all subject fields.

One sixth-grade class, whose teacher has been most active on the Committee, took the in-service teachers on exploration trips on their school grounds. Each committee of children had six teachers and used the method of discovery with them. One group of children clustered around an old oak stump could be heard asking the teachers, "How old do think this tree was when it was cut down?" "Were there any years of drought when it was growing?" and "How many years did it grow after it was first used as a fence post?"

The Committee prepared three filmstrips with sound recordings which can be used by teachers to help plan, carry out, evaluate, and follow up on lessons which have been carried on in the out-of-doors. One is at the third-grade level and shows how the class makes use of the school yard each day in its units of work. A sixth-grade class is making use of a city park to introduce a unit in social studies, and an eighth-grade class goes on a day trip to a neighboring lake and woods for its culminating unit on conservation.

Another area in which the Committee is able to give assistance to teachers is helping plan for outdoor experiences and accompanying them on the trip as resource people. One such trip was made by a ninth-grade class which was culminating a unit of study. The class spent the day at a well-known woods forty miles from the city. This group had spent a long time in preparation for the trip with their various committees carrying out all necessary research and other assignments.

When the beaver committee actually found the dam and house and was able to see the chips at the tree stumps and tooth marks on the branches, its reading and studying took on real meaning. When the compass committee led the group through deep woods to a lovely stream that it had located on the geodetic map, their appreciation was all the keener for the accuracy of the Sylva compass and their ability to read a map and follow the compass.

It is such experiences as these that makes learning take on real meaning and gives the challenge to youth which is so often lacking in school. Teachers and students alike experience the thrill that comes when the greatest laboratory of all becomes an integral part of the school program.

A State Conservation Workshop

Cooperation is the basis for the seventeen years of continued operation of the Ohio Conservation Laboratory. At the present time, the five state universities, the State Department of Education, and the Division of Wildlife of the Department of Natural Resources are cooperating in sponsoring a workshop that offers undergraduate or graduate credit.

Five full-time instructors and a part-time shop assistant comprise the instructional staff that develops the basic program before the opening of the five-week session. The students and staff cooperatively develop many of the daily programs designed to give the individual every opportunity for improvement in various areas of his own choosing. As the previous preparation and experience of the students varies widely, the program is designed to provide a maximum of flexibility in meeting individual needs. This is achieved by working with small groups in the field and by numerous individual conferences.

Basic instruction is given to all students in soil and water relationships, biotic resources, non-renewable resources, demography, and teaching methods and techniques. While some of the teaching is done indoors, most of it is performed in the out-of-doors, either on organized field trips of a full or half-day duration or by working with small groups in our "outdoor laboratory." This laboratory is the area surrounding one of the lakes of the famed Muskingum Watershed Conservancy District. A fully winterized former NYA camp on the shore of beautiful Leesville Lake is the facility that has housed the Ohio Conservation Laboratory for the past fourteen years.

Four members of the full-time staff are faculty members of universities. All are proficient in general conservation instruction and each is a specialist in one or more fields. The fifth staff member is the supervisor of conservation for the State Department of Education. During all major field trips and for certain sessions on specific topics, a number of resource personnel from Federal or state agencies and other organiaztions work closely with the staff. All-day tours take the students to the U.S. Department of Agriculture, Coshocton Soil and Water Experiment Station; through part of the Muskingum Watershed Conservancy District; and to the coal strip-mine area of Eastern Ohio. Half-day trips include a farm under the Soil Conservation Service plan; a forest area under proper management; and a local school yard. The latter site provides students with a number of experiences that may be applied, with modifications, to their own teaching situation.

A unique feature of the laboratory is a small shop, well equipped with hand tools. Students are invited, but not required, to construct their own teaching aids. Over the years, a remarkable number of articles have been produced. They vary from a simple project, such as an insect spreading board or plant press, to complex electrical quiz boards and beautiful display cases. Flannel boards, tree sections, terrariums, papier mache models, insect nets, posters, ozalid and smoke prints, run-off boxes, clinometers, and a host of other aids have been taken back to the classrooms and put to immediate use.

Many of the teachers attend the laboratory with some financial assistance furnished by organizations having an interest in promoting conservation education. These teachers not only become aware of conservation problems, but also realize the necessity for action by the schools. They likewise recognize that the out-of-doors, in many instances, is better than any classroom for the teaching of certain skills and understandings about man and his environment. What is more, they feel qualified to supplement their classroom activities through these outdoor experiences. In this respect they can contribute much to the total outdoor education program.

College-Sponsored Workshops and Off-Campus Courses

Indiana University

One of the particular needs of teachers with responsibilities for outdoor education is experience in the outdoor setting that will provide a background of outdoor knowledge and some skill in techniques of working with children in this setting. Several colleges and universities have developed workshops and courses with this need in mind. Two types of such off-campus courses are given by the Department of Recreation of Indiana University at the Bradford Woods Outdoor Education Area, a 2,300-acre forest located twenty-six miles north of the Bloomington campus.

A fifteen-day course in school-camp program activities is conducted in the period between the end of the spring session and the beginning of the summer session. The course, for which graduate credit is given, is conducted in an outdoor setting with numerous opportunities for field trips, conservation projects, work on a nature trail, collecting, demonstration cook-outs, visits to camps in the area, camp construction, etc. Lectures and discussions center around program skills and the philosophy of outdoor education. Each member of the group works on an individual project related to the specific teaching situation in which he is involved.

The primary purpose of this course is to help the teacher develop skill in handling school groups out-of-doors. In any such group of teachers, there is considerable variation in background and skill in outdoor activities. It is expected that teachers will supplement this course with content courses in various subject fields if they have not previously done so.

An eight-week summer session for graduate students follows this course at Bradford Woods. During the summer, several outdoor-related courses are offered. One of them is particularly concerned with outdoor education. This course, of five weeks' duration, involves a period of training followed by the actual conducting of a six-day day camp for children from the Indiana University Elementary School. The first three weeks of the course are spent in developing the program for the day camp, and three afternoons a week for each of these three weeks are spent in the camp itself. All aspects of the program are discussed, and members of the class get acquainted with the area and its potentialities for educational purposes. Supplies and equipment are gathered, and the area is made ready for the camp. Responsibilities for the day camp are then divided. Some members of the class serve as counselors; one assumes responsibility for health and safety; another keeps the financial records; another assumes charge of the evening programs; another arranges transportation; and so on through all the responsibilities of the camp. Since there are usually twenty to twenty-five members of the class and only about sixty children in the camp, not all the graduate students can be used as counselors. People with special science skills or other program specialties are used to develop programs in these fields.

Before the camp opens, meetings are held with classroom teachers in an effort to coordinate the camp program with the school program. When the camp begins, one of the teachers serves as camp director. Other teachers attend the camp and participate in the program, but the major responsibility rests with the graduate students.

Following the six-day camp period, evaluation of the camp is made by the campers themselves, teachers, parents, and members of the graduate class. An annual report of the experience is prepared and made available to interested people.

Both of these courses are based on the assumptions that direct experience in the out-of-doors and in working with children in the out-of-doors are among the most significant means of developing leadership for outdoor education. In addition to these two graduate courses, Indiana University is one of the sponsors of the annual Conference on Interpretation Programs, held for three days each spring at Bradford Woods. Though intended primarily for naturalists, many people engaged in school camping attend the workshop and contribute to its program.

Other Workshops

National Camp

National Camp is a center for the preparation of advanced leadership in outdoor education and camping. This national training center was founded in 1940, and is operated by the Outdoor Education Association, Incorporated. National Camp's location in the Pocono Mountains of Pennsylvania, near Matamoras, overlooks a part of the beautiful Delaware Valley. Comprising a large track, nearly 1,000 acres of woodland and meadows adjacent to thousands of acres of state forest, the site offers an abundance of wildlife and geographical phenomena.

The purposes of this unique training center are: (1) to give impetus to the concept of outdoor education and school camping projected in the early '30's; (2) to prepare advanced leaders for the program; (3) to promote education and school camping through special conferences, workshops, institutes, demonstrations, and projects; and (4) to operate a camp for boys and girls as a laboratory for observation, study, and research by those who attend the leadership training program.

As the interest in outdoor education and school camping has increased, hundreds of teachers, college faculty members, administrators, and camp and other youth-serving agency personnel have attended regular sessions and institutes during the summer sessions. As greater numbers of schools and organizations turn to the out-of-doors for a more realistic approach to meet the present-day needs of youth, there is an ever-increasing demand for improved leadership.

The program at National Camp is devoted to advanced study and practice. Participants are helped to develop specific plans for their own schools, colleges, organizations, or communities. The summer session is a practical field course in administration and leadership of outdoor education, with special emphasis on the development of year-round programs. Students learn through many different kinds of field trips, group and individual conferences, general sessions, research, and participation in all phases of camp living.

Construction of different types of shelters and equipment, exploration trips, overnight camping, menu planning and food marketing, nature and conservation activities, and many kinds of field trips are among the practical experiences offered. In addition to this wide range of experiences, assistance is given to each student concerning his own problem. The large and very complete library is available for use in study and research.

Since the founding of National Camp, many hundreds of key leaders in this new phase of education have gone out to schools, colleges, and communities in all parts of the country and instituted programs in outdoor education and school camping.

Audubon Camps

The consensus of most educators is that the best kind of learning is through direct experience. The National Audubon Society applies this technique to the teaching of natural science in various camp locations throughout the country.

A critical look at the teacher-supply situation brings abundant evidence of the increasing numbers who are seeking information, understanding, and knowledge in this field. Thus, Audubon Camps came into existence because, generally speaking, state teachers colleges and normal schools did not train student teachers to present nature and conservation subjects effectively, or to integrate these subjects with existing curriculums. In addition, the Camp programs were designed to build a majority public opinion favoring wise use of natural resources.

Located in Maine, Connecticut, Wisconsin, and California, Audubon Camps are operated for teachers, youth leaders, and others with a professional and/or avocational interest in nature and conservation. Members of Audubon Camp teaching staffs are selected for their background in a specialized field of biological science and for their ability as all-round naturalists. They interpret nature in terms of process. Interested in *what* is there, their chief concern lies with "What goes on there."

Because participation is an effective learning technique, total enrollment in the Camps is limited and groups in the field number only around a dozen. This makes possible the free and easy exchange of ideas and experiences and readily breaks down the fears that inhibit people from voicing questions when in large gatherings. Of equal importance, the small group provides the opportunity for the leader to take *time* to explain and to reiterate until understanding is achieved. This develops a feeling of security on the part of the individual and establishes the important realization that repetition is a vital though often minimized ingredient in learning at all ages.

It is interesting to note that Audubon Camp programs do not practice specialization nor play to the pitfalls of highlighting and comparing one experience against another. Rather, they seek to take what is at hand, be it sea, shore, meadow, forest, or mountain, and utilize to the fullest what it has to tell. No attempt is made during a single session to tell *all* there is to know about any one subject. Those who come with knowledge and background in a given field find the intriguing opportunity to broaden horizons in other areas. The uncertainties of the newcomer who is doubtful of being able to understand because of a lack of scientific background are immediately dissipated because the program is so varied and does not require tests or examinations. For the in-betweens, the generalists who have dabbled in all fields yet never seen them as a related whole, there lies the opportunity to develop important new over-all concepts. It is the moulding together of such widely divergent interests and backgrounds into common understanding that makes for a lasting learning process. The very lack of over-emphasized highlights removes the necessity of comparisons between what happened on each consecutive day, and sends campers home unable to pinpoint any one experience against another.

They recall that the program as a whole was enjoyable, building a reservoir of meaningful memories and resources to be drawn upon in the future.

Lastly, and perhaps the most telling accomplishment of an Audubon Camp experience, is the transformation in two short weeks of strangers into friends with a common bond of interest in nature and conservation and the determination to *do* something. With the program emphasis on *all* living things, their interdependence on each other and relationship to us as human beings, the word ecology takes on hithertofore untold meaning, resulting in a fraternity whose unity of purpose is the conservation of natural resources. This, like the enlarging snowball rolling downhill, is the aim of all Audubon Camps.

Red Cross Courses

The American National Red Cross and, more specifically, its educational services are able to provide the professional teacher the opportunity to receive in-service training in first aid, water safety, small craft safety, and home nursing. Graded courses in first aid, water safety, and small craft safety, designed to meet the needs of all, on whatever level desired, are available through more than 3,700 Red Cross chapters. Instructor courses in these subjects are probably of most importance to professional teachers. In these courses, taught by designated representatives of the Red Cross, the emphasis is on the "how" of teaching rather than on the development of personal skills.

A special course, designed for professional teachers, leading to an instructor's certificate in first aid has been prepared for teachers who have completed the standard and advanced first aid courses. Teachers who have completed the American Red Cross senior life saving course are eligible to enroll in the water safety instructor course. Instructor courses in small craft safety, including boating, canoeing, and sailing, have been developed for those who have passed the basic courses in these activities.

Teachers working with physically limited students will find the instructor course in swimming for the handicapped to be of particular interest. Authorized Red Cross water safety instructors are permitted to enroll in the course for certification. Teachers who are not water safety instructors, but who express a desire for this type of training, may audit the course.

Instructor courses in first aid, water safety, and small craft safety are taught in Red Cross chapters, in many colleges and universities, and in Red Cross aquatic schools. There is no fee for any Red Cross course.

Another course of interest and one that is open to teachers of home economics, physical education, and related subjects is the home nursing instructor course. Teachers completing the course are authorized to teach certificated courses in care of the sick and injured.

Teachers who desire to enroll in one or more Red Cross courses are encouraged to contact the nearest Red Cross chapter. The address can be found in the local telephone directory.

CHAPTER V

A Look Into the Future

THERE can be little doubt that education in the outdoors is a timely development in the American school system. There is widespread acceptance by schools and colleges of the values implicit in using *all* community resources, including the out-of-doors, in the educative process. In conjunction with the phenomenal growth of outdoor education programs during the past two decades, this forecasts unprecedented developments in the future.

It is clear that good learning and the outdoors are inseparable—that more complete use of the outdoor laboratory is necessary as a means of relating man to his natural environment—to give him "roots in the soil" in this atomic age. The simple, but fundamental pronouncements, testimony of experience and observations which is contained in this book, constitutes a broad charter for outdoor education which includes the following points:

1. Education in the outdoors, through direct experience, is in keeping with the best that is now known about how the individual learns.

2. Today's living, with its large population centers and automation, has deprived many children and youth of contact with the land. Schools must, therefore, provide outdoor learning opportunities in order that they may renew this contact as a normal part of growing up.

3. The emerging community school—the instrument for serving those learning and living needs of present-day society with which education has been charged—makes maximum use of all community resources, including the out-of-doors.

4. Achievement of the purposes and objectives of this ever-changing institution can be completely realized only through a community curriculum—the sum total of all learning situations provided by the many groups and agencies.

5. There is more emphasis on "creative education" that helps people find satisfactions—many of them in the outdoors—during the increasing amount of off-the-job time at their disposal.

6. Outdoor education is a broad term—not a discipline nor a subject-matter field—that includes those learning experiences indigenous to the natural environment and the skills, appreciations, and attitudes necessary for maximum satisfactions and enjoyment in outdoor pursuits.

Students improve and protect the land for the future.

7. Knowledge, skills, attitudes, and appreciations that are acquired *in* and *for* the outdoors are integral parts of general education and are included in appropriate places in many disciplines, school subjects, and activities.

8. Teachers should be equally competent to teach *in* and *outside* the classroom, wherever the environment is most conducive to the desired learnings.

9. Techniques and methods basic to good teachings are equally effective in both kinds of "classrooms," indoor and out.

10. There are many settings suitable for learning in and for the outdoors—camps, parks, forests, farms, gardens, and open spaces.

11. All schools and community agencies charged with the responsibility for the education of children have available to them some type of outdoor setting suitable for learning.

12. Through cooperative planning at local, state, and Federal levels, more adequate facilities, leadership, and equipment for outdoor education may be made available. This will secure more efficient use of the tax dollar by eliminating needless duplication of effort.

13. If *all* people are to come into full possession of their outdoor heritage, it is of paramount importance that there must be inter-departmental and inter-agency cooperation at the local, state, and Federal levels.

14. Some of the basic needs of youth, unmet by schools with traditional programs, can be satisfied by the community school. If this challenge is not met, it will become necessary, by default, for other agencies than the school to assume this responsibility. An example may be found in the work-learning experiences on the land for older youth—as furnished by the CCC. Education needs to grasp and hold militant leadership in providing such programs under the jurisdiction of appropriate local and state educational and conservation authorities.

Complete realization of the heritage of every citizen to experience the physical, mental, and spiritual benefits from God-given natural resources will be reflected in broader and richer educational opportunities for which schools have a major responsibility. A community school that is truly the embodiment of the yearnings of the people for the education of their children and for themselves is a service agency in which the function of the school administration and teachers is to help people learn. The future will find teachers and learners increasingly going to the outdoors to achieve broad educational goals and specific classroom objectives. Classrooms and school sites, such as found in "park schools," will facilitate the smooth flow in and out of school buildings into all the appropriate open spaces of the immediate and greater community—to camps, in forests, on farms.

As children and youth find new and exciting adventures in learning outdoors, the label of the leader will matter little—whether it be educator, conservationist, recreationist, youth leader, or minister—for all are teachers in the broadest sense. Youth will become benefactors to the land, and the association with mother earth will be good for our junior citizens as they find opportunities to improve and protect the land.

The process will not only help in the conservation of natural resources; it will also serve to prevent human "erosion." Such education is not only essential to the "growing up" process, it is also a balm to the tensions of adulthood and adds a glow to the later years. These things, envisioned for the future, will give youth a stake in the land which will be reflected in the kind of citizenship that is the essence of democracy.

Resources

NATIONAL ORGANIZATIONS AND THEIR MAGAZINES

American Association for Health, Physical Education, and Recreation, 1201 Sixteenth Street, N. W., Washington, D. C. *The Journal of Health, Physical Education, Recreation.*

American Camping Association, Inc., Bradford Woods, Martinsville, Indiana. *Camping Magazine-Conservation in Camping,* and other publications on camping.

American Forestry Association, 919 Seventeenth Street, N. W., Washington, D. C. *American Forests.*

American Museum of Natural History, Seventy-Seventh Street and Central Park West, New York, New York. *Natural History.*

American Nature Association, 1214 Sixteenth Street, N. W., Washington, D. C. *Nature Magazine.*

American Youth Hostels, Inc., 6 East 39th Street, New York, New York.

Appalachian Mountain Club, 5 Joy Street, Boston, Massachusetts.

Audubon Society of Canada, 177 Jarvis Street, Toronto 2, Ontario, Canada. *Canadian Nature.*

Boy Scouts of America, 2 Park Avenue, New York, New York. *Boy's Life.*

Camp Fire Girls, 16 East 48th Street, New York 17, New York.

4-H Clubs, Extension Service, U. S. Department of Agriculture, Washington 25, D. C.

Friends of the Land, 1368 N. High Street, Columbus, Ohio. *The Land.*

Garden Clubs of America, 15 East 56th Street, New York, New York.

Girl Scouts of U. S. A., 155 East 44th Street, New York 17, New York.

Izaak Walton League of America, LaSalle Hotel, Chicago, Illinois. *Outdoor America.*

National Association of Angling and Casting Clubs, 960 Paul Brown Building, St. Louis 1, Missouri. *The Creel.*

National Audubon Society, Inc., 1006 Fifth Avenue, New York, New York. *Audubon Magazine.*

National Council of State Garden Clubs, 500 Fifth Avenue, New York 16, New York.

National Geographic Society, 1146 Sixteenth Street, Washington 6, D. C. *National Geographic Magazine.*

National Rifle Association, 1600 Rhode Island Avenue, N. W., Washington, D. C. *The American Rifleman.*

National Wildlife Federation, 232 Carroll Street, N. W., Takoma Park 12, Washington, D. C.

Young Men's Christian Association, 291 Broadway, New York, New York.

Young Women's Christian Association, 600 Lexington Avenue, New York, New York.

SERVICE ORGANIZATIONS

*(These organizations provide many helpful materials, lists
of which may be obtained upon request)*

American National Red Cross, Seventeenth and D Streets, N. W., Washington, D. C.

Associated Fishing Tackle Manufacturers, Bond Building, Washington, D. C.

Athletic Institute, 209 South State Street, Chicago, Illinois.

Junior Safety Institute, 230 N. Michigan Avenue, Suite A, Chicago Illinois.

Outboard Boating Club of America, 307 North Michigan Avenue, Chicago, Illinois.

National Recreation Association, 8 West Eighth Street, New York, New York.

Sport Fishing Institute, Bond Building, Washington 5, D. C.

Sporting Arms and Ammunitions Manufacturers' Institute, 250 East 43rd Street, New York, New York.

SELECTED BIBLIOGRAPHY

Allen, Shirley W. *Conserving Natural Resources.* New York: McGraw-Hill Book Company, Inc. 1955.

American Association for Health, Physical Education, and Recreation (AAHPER). *Administrative Problems in Health, Physical Education, and Recreation.* Chapter 10, "Camping Education in the Secondary School." Washington, D. C.: The Association. 1953.

AAHPER. *Children in Focus,* the 1954 Yearbook. Washington, D. C.: The Association. 1954.

AAHPER. *Fitness for Secondary-School Youth.* pp. 85-123. Chapter 4. Washington, D. C.: The Association. 1956.

AAHPER. *Shooting and Firearms Education.* Washington, D. C.: The Association. 1956.

American Association of School Administrators. *Conservation Education.* Washington, D. C.: The Association. 1951.

American National Red Cross. *Canoeing.* Garden City, New York: Doubleday and Company, Inc. 1956.

Athletic Institute. *Planning Facilities for Health, Physical Education, and Recreation.* Chicago: The Athletic Institute.

Athletic Institute. *The Recreation Program.* Chicago: The Athletic Institute. 1954.

Benson, Reuel A.; Jacob A. Goldberg; and others. *The Camp Counselor.* New York: McGraw-Hill Book Company, Inc. 1951.

Burns, Gerald. *Programs of the Modern Camp.* New York: Prentice-Hall, Inc. 1954.

Camp Sites and Facilities. New York: Boy Scouts of America.

Clarke, James M. *California's Pilot Project in Outdoor Education.* Stanford, California: The Stanford University Press. 1951.

Clarke, James M. *Public School Camping*. Stanford, California: The Stanford University Press. 1951.

Damon, G. E. *Gun-Fun with Safety*. Huntington, West Virginia: Standard Publications, Inc. 1947.

Dimock, Hedley S., and others. *Administration of the Modern Camp*. New York: Association Press. 1948.

Donaldson, George W. *School Camping*. New York: Association Press. 1952.

Elliott, Russ. *Your Shotgun vs. You*. Kansas City, Missouri: Brown-White-Lowell Press. 1955.

The Fisherman's Handbook. Oxford, Ohio: The Fisherman's Press, Inc. 1955.

Friet, Edwin L., and Peterson, Del G. *Design for Outdoor Education*. Yakima, Washington: P. S. Printers, Inc. 1956.

Gilliland, John W. *School Camping, A Frontier of Curriculum Improvement*. Washington, D. C.: Association for Supervision and Curriculum Development. 1954.

Gilliland, John W. *A Study of Administrative Factors in Establishing a Program of School Camping*, Doctoral Thesis, New York University. 1949.

Hammett, Catherine T., and Musselman, Virginia. *The Camp Program Book*. New York: Association Press. 1954.

Hillcourt, William. *Field Book of Nature Activities*. New York: G. P. Putnam's Sons. 1950.

Irwin, Frank L. *The Theory of Camping: An Introduction to Camping in Education*. New York: A. S. Barnes and Company. 1950.

Kelley, Earl C. *Education for What Is Real*. New York: Harper and Brothers, Publishers. 1947.

Kjellstrom, Bjorn. *Be Expert with Map and Compass*. New York: American Orienteering Service, 220 Fifth Avenue. 1955.

Leopold, Aldo. *A Sand County Almanac*. New York: Oxford University Press. 1949.

Mackintosh, Helen K. *Camping and Outdoor Experiences in the School Program*. Washington, D. C.: Superintendent of Documents, United States Government Printing Office. 1947.

Mac-Millan, Dorothy Lou. *School Camping and Outdoor Education*. Dubuque, Iowa: Wm. C. Brown Company. 1956.

Manley, Helen, and M. F. Drury. *Education Through School Camping*. St. Louis: C. V. Mosby Company. 1952.

Michigan State University. *Nature Trails and Labels*. Park Management Bulletin Number 5. East Lansing: The University. 1957.

Michigan State University. *Outdoor Education—A Way to Better Living*. Park Management Bulletin Number 6. East Lansing: The University. 1957.

Mitchell, Viola, and Crawford, Ida. *Camp Counseling*. Philadelphia: W. B. Saunders Publishing Company. 1950.

National Association of Biology Teachers. *Handbook for Teaching Conservation Resource Use.* Ann Arbor, Michigan: The Association. 1955.

National Association of Secondary-School Principals. "Camping and Outdoor Education," edited by L. B. Sharp and E. DeAlton Partridge, *Bulletin of the National Association of Secondary-School Principals,* 31:147, May, 1947. (*Out of print.*)

Olsen, E. G., editor. *School and Community,* "The Community School Camp," by Julian W. Smith. New York: Prentice Hall. 1954.

Outdoor Education Association, Inc. *Extending Education Through Camping.* New York: The Association (With the New York City Board of Education) . 1948.

Peterson, Gunnar, editor. *The Outing Club Handbook.* Chicago: The editor, George Williams College. 1955.

Salamon, Julian H. *Camp Site Development.* New York: Girl Scouts of U. S. A. 1948.

Smith County Youth Foundation. *Camp Tyler.* Tyler, Texas: Story-Wright Printing Company.

Smith, Julian W. *Outdoor Education.* Washington, D. C.: American Association for Health, Physical Education, and Recreation (In cooperation with the Classroom Teachers Association) . 1956.

Thurston, Lee M. *Community School Camping.* Lansing: Indiana State Superintendent of Public Instruction. 1950.

Thurston, Lee M. *Community School Camps* (A Guide for Development) . Lansing: Indiana State Superintendent of Public Instruction.

Thurston, Lee M. *A Community School Work-Learn Camp.* Lansing: Indiana State Superintendent of Public Instruction. 1951.

United States Office of Education. *Camping and Outdoor Experiences in the School Program,* U. S. Office of Education Bulletin, 1947, No. 4. Washington, D. C.: Superintendent of Documents, United States Government Printing Office.

Using Resources Wisely. Albany: New York State Education Department. 1956.

Vinal, William Gould. *Nature Recreation,* Group Guidance for the Outdoors. New York: McGraw-Hill Book Company. 1940.

Vinal, William Gould. *The Outdoor Schoolroom for Outdoor Living.* Cohasset, Massachusetts: Vinehall. 1952.

AUDIO-VISUAL AIDS

(Films on Outdoor Recreation)

Federal government agencies, such as U. S. Department of Agriculture, Soil Conservation, and Forest Service

Regional and state offices of the soil conservation service

State departments of conservation

University film libraries

State University Extension Service
National Audubon Society Photo and Film Department
Film rental libraries

FEDERAL GOVERNMENT

Many agencies of the Federal government publish both free and sales literature which is useful for recreation program planning as it relates to the agency fields. The Superintendent of Documents, Washington 25, D. C., will furnish selected lists of sales publications. All orders should be addressed to the Superintendent of Documents address rather than to the agency.

In addition, many of the agencies make direct free distribution of leaflets, publications lists, charts, posters, *etc.,* upon request. Several of the agencies lend films and other visual aids, or issue lists of their films which may be rented from film libraries. The U. S. Office of Education issues a periodical list of selected government films, and another of film libraries.

The following list includes agencies most likely to have material useful in outdoor recreation. All agencies are addressed: Washington 25, D. C.

U. S. Department of Agriculture (composite publications list)
    Forest Service
    Soil Conservation Service
    Extension Service
The Smithsonian Institute
U. S. Department of Health, Education, and Welfare
    Office of Education
    Public Health Service
U. S. Department of the Interior
    National Park Service
    Bureau of Reclamation
    Bureau of Land Management
    Bureau of Indian Affairs
    Bureau of Mines
    U. S. Geological Survey
    Fish and Wildlife Service

STATE GOVERNMENT

State Department of Conservation
State Department of Public Instruction
State University
State Agricultural College
State 4-H Clubs (Extension Service, State College of Agriculture)
State Department of Health

COUNTY

County agricultural agent or local agricultural county extension office
County forester or game manager

LOCAL OR COMMUNITY

Game wardens
Forest rangers
Park rangers
Soil conservation service technicians
Soil conservation district personnel
Agriculture teachers in high schools and vocational schools

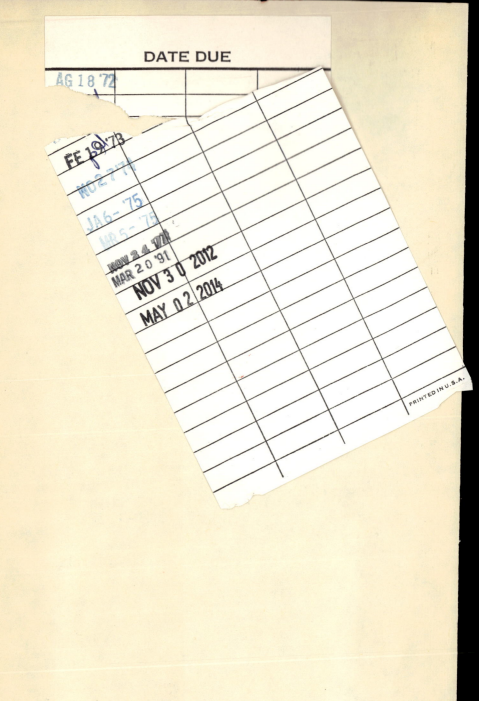